D1176888

ELIMINATED

ELIMINATED

what to expect when the unexpected happens

L. Patrick Bush

Have you ever been faced with a transition in your employment? Even if you suspect it might happen or if you are given some notice, the effects of a job loss can be devastating. Typically, out-placement services, recruiters, friends and family will provide you with advice on behaviors and techniques, but no one prepares you for the emotional effects. Until now.

First paperback edition December 2018
Book design by Danielle Johnson

ISBN 9781791556150 (paperback)
ISBN 9781983283154 (ebook)

Published by Kindle Direct Publishing

Dedicated to my wife Debbie who was never judgmental as I learned first-hand what it was like to be eliminated. To my daughter Nicole who completed the first edit of the manuscript; to my son Larry who called me every day when I was looking for work; to my son Justin who supported me emotionally during the hardest times; to my daughter Anna who never complained when we had to make some significant budget cuts; and to all the people who have been in this same position and shared their stories with me.

INTRODUCTION

I decided to write this book to shine a light on a subject that wasn't being discussed. When I got my head straight after my first job elimination, I started talking with other men and women with similar experiences. I was shocked at how the process was always the same. I knew what had worked for me and I began to have those conversations with others who were in transition. I didn't focus on the behaviors (e.g. networking, job boards) or the techniques (e.g. LinkedIn, resume), I focused on the attitude. I found that most people – including myself – focused on behaviors and techniques. There were plenty of tips and techniques that dealt with prospecting for a new job and how to interview. No one focused on attitude and NO ONE talked about the emotional side of the job loss. This was a problem because eighty percent of the success in finding that new job is attitude.

The emotional side of the job loss and the attitude of opening that new chapter in your career requires us to be vulnerable. As human beings, we do not want to show vulnerability. Job eliminations will continue with Generation X as the next group when they begin to hit their 50's and 60's. It's too early to tell if the process will continue with the millennials or if they will move from one job to another so frequently that this won't be an issue. Or, the millennial generation may cope with job loss differently and show their vulnerability. Maybe job loss will become so prevalent that it becomes the new normal. For the foreseeable future, job elimination will continue and the effect on the person eliminated will be traumatic.

Over the years, acquaintances who had experienced job elimination either gravitated to me or were referred to me because, unfortunately, I'm an expert at job elimination. Now, by default, I have heard more stories than almost anyone else. Maybe some counselors or priests have heard more stories, but they probably don't have firsthand experience. I decided to share what works and how to manage through the process. As bad as someone thinks their story is, I probably have a "topper."

The phenomena started in mid-1990 when companies found they could reorganize and not be subject to discrimination lawsuits in terminating employees. Prior to that, most companies were cautious regarding "protected classes" of employees and would make exceptions to avoid legal proceeding or predatory practices. The older employees were probably at the top of the wage scale, had more accrued benefits (PTO, shares, bonuses) and more company-sponsored costs (e.g. healthcare) than other employees. The question was how to terminate these protected class of employees, reset the costing by hiring other younger, less-experienced and cheaper employees and not get sued for age discrimination. The employee-at-will statement that is included in many applications today may be glossed over when the applicant is completing an application after the hiring offer has been made. With this statement, an employer can terminate an employee for good cause, bad cause or no cause at all. There are three major exceptions to the employee-at-will doctrine: public policy exception (whereby there is a well-established public policy within the state. Missouri recognizes this when the public policy is from the State constitution and statutes.); an implied-contract exception (whereby an employer may make written or oral representations of job security. Some states do not recognize this); and covenant-of-good faith exception (whereby an employer's personnel decisions are subject to a "just cause" standard. Some states again do not recognize this exception.)

A court in Missouri in 1985 reviewed wrongful discharge cases that were reported between 1977 and 1984 and concluded:

As many of the decided cases illustrate, the burden of the at-will employment doctrine seems to be falling most heavily and harshly upon professional and upper- and middle-level employees.
[Footnote that cites 15 cases] They have the least protection. Most are at-will employees and few have job security through union or individually-negotiated contracts. They have the most to lose, frequently being the long-term employees who have the greatest responsibility and substantial investment in and the highest expectations from their careers. Often, they are at an age when replacement of their life and medical insurance programs and their retirement plans are difficult or impossible.
(Footnote)
Boyle v. Vista Eyewear, Inc., 700 S.W.2d 859, 877-878 (Mo.App. 1985).

Most employees who have been with a company for many years probably do not remember the application they completed when they were first hired. The employee-at-will provision cuts both ways and employees are not required to provide notice when they quit. If there is an employment agreement, this could be spelled out that notice is required. Most employees believe they "owe" the employer notice, but the employer may not feel the same way in a job elimination.

Due to these provisions and the move toward more at-will employment, men and women in their 50's and 60's find themselves suddenly eliminated even after receiving outstanding performance reviews. Most often, the elimination is not anticipated, and the employee is blindsided. This can be especially traumatic because it is not anticipated. Depending on the position with the company and the length of service, we can be duped into a sense of security. We have a version of "happy ears" where we may ignore signs of trouble ahead or think we will not be a part of the cutbacks.

In this book, I present the story of Jack, a fictional character that is an amalgamation of many stories shared with me over many years. After Jack's story, I provide some practical advice on managing this process and getting to emotional health and balance. At the end, I share my own story. I've told my story countless times one-on-one but never to a group of people that I do not know. I share it because I have experienced the same process that many of you are experiencing now or have experienced. I share it now because you need to know that it will all work out. I had to learn to let go and let God take over. This was the hardest lesson of my life, but it works. Funny how my wife Debbie knew all along, but I ignored all of the signs and always thought I was in control. What an idiot.

If you haven't been through something like this, share it with someone who may be going through this now. Most of us don't want to discuss a job elimination. But just knowing that other people go through the same process can be encouraging and having practical advice to move forward can be motivating. Enjoy!

JACK

the blindside

A morning person, Jack Thompson always arrived at the office before most people were out of bed. He had his regular routine, nothing fancy. He'd stop at a QT to get coffee and then onto the highway for the drive to the office when he wasn't headed to the airport. That was a normal day. He often traveled and would select flights with the lowest prices which meant being at the airport for the "O'dark thirty" flight. He viewed his expenses as if he were spending HIS own money, and he always tried to travel before or after the normal workday. Some of his peers in similar positions would never do that. They worked for large companies and didn't think twice about expenses.

Wagner was a small, privately-held business and the President & CEO, Bill Wagner, was also the owner and Jack's boss. Jack had worked for larger companies, but he had settled in at Wagner. He liked the smaller, family-feel of the business where, when you made decisions, you could get immediate feedback on the change. He understood that small, privately-held companies were more sensitive to issues and an owner could make unilateral decisions that might not always be favorable for the employees. In his ten years with the company, Wagner had grown from just under $25MM to almost $100MM and the profitability had also increased.

Today, everything changed.

As usual, Jack arrived early. He logged onto his email and the CRM system, updated his dashboards and reviewed how the salespeople were doing. He had one-on-ones scheduled with a couple of the salespeople and he wanted to prepare.

At 9:00 AM Bill Wagner, the owner, stopped by Jack's office.

"Hey, what's up?" Jack asked.

"Not much. Wanted to see how you're doing. Where are we on those two new opportunities?"

"I'm getting updates this morning. If I read the tea leaves, we have a pretty good shot for at least one of them. They're not huge, but they all count toward our goal."

"How are we doing against goal?"

"I think we're going to be short. Some of the opportunities that were in the forecast didn't close, and we don't have enough in the pipeline to make up the difference."

"I'd like to go over the sales and financials this afternoon, Jack. Say, 4:00 PM. Will that work?"

"Absolutely. I have some one-on-ones today and I should have updated numbers I can share."

"Good, see you at four."

The updates from the one-on-ones weren't good. The two new opportunities were likely going to be awarded to competitors.

Renewals didn't fall under Jack; they were the responsibility of the VP of Operations and the VP had been blindsided when a long-standing customer switched companies without any warning. It wasn't the last blindside that would happen today.

Jack arrived just before 4:00 PM at Bill's office. Bill was on the phone, so he waived Jack in and pointed to a small conference table. Jack sat down, with the latest sales numbers and forecasts. He placed a copy on the table for Bill. Bill finished his call, walked past the conference table to the office door and closed it. He sat down with the copies in front of him. *Not a good sign.* Closing the door always meant bad news. Something was up.

"Jack, listen. I know the sales team is doing everything they can to close some business, but it won't make an impact this year. We budgeted our expenses based on a revenue number that we are assured now won't be met. We have to make some difficult choices so I'm going to have to "right-size" the company based on the new revenue forecasts. That right-sizing means eliminating some positions and yours is one that I have to eliminate. You've done a great job here, but we have to reduce expenses, and this is the quickest way for us to get back on track."

Wow. I'm only an expense? Really? I have been just a warm body, taking up space. I guess any trained circus monkey could do this job.

"So," Jack managed to stutter, "Who is taking...over the sales responsibility?"

"I will have to step in and have the salespeople report directly to me. It'll be more time-consuming for me, but that's what we'll have to do." He paused, his lips pursed. "Jack, you know this isn't easy for me. You've been a major part of our growth over the last ten years, but I don't really have any other choice."

"When...when will this be effective?"

"Immediately. Today will be your last day. Beth will come in to discuss your unpaid vacation, and how COBRA will work."

Immediately? Last day? "What about my shares from the share plan? I hit the targets over the past five years, and I have 200,000 shares. Do I get any value for those?"

"I'm afraid not, Jack. That plan was developed to retain our top talent so they would share in the profits if and when the company was sold or there was a 51.0% change in control. If you leave before the company sells, there's no value and you forfeit your shares."

Jack's heart was beating so fast that he could barely think. "Wow. You mean I worked for the last five years to achieve the goals and be rewarded with shares that get stripped away just like that?"

"I know it seems like that, but that's the way these plans are written."

"What about severance?"

"Yes, what I worked out for all employees is to receive one week of pay for each year they've been with the company, so you'll receive ten weeks of pay."

He opened his mouth but couldn't speak. Finally, he blurted, "Incredible. I gave up spending time with my family; traveled way too much; worked nights and weekends sometimes more than 70 hours a week; was loyal to Wagner almost to a fault; didn't pursue other opportunities; received outstanding performance reviews and in the end, it all means nothing. I'm just an expense that has to be eliminated."

There was a knock at the door. Bill said, "I've asked Beth to come in and she will cover your termination benefits."

Beth, the Human Resource Director, was a tall, attractive, middle-aged woman with a bit of gray streaking her hair. She strolled into Bill's office carrying a Bankers Box with no lid and a bright red folder. She sat down across from Bill and opened the folder, explained how severance, vacation, and PTO will be paid and provided the forms for COBRA for ongoing healthcare coverage. Beth slipped all of the forms for Jack into the red folder and placed it in the bottom of the Bankers Box.

"Jack," she said, "we should take a walk down to your office so you can remove your personal items and then I will escort you out."

As they all stood up, Jack said, "Thanks, Beth. Why do I feel like I got caught stealing something?"

"It's company policy. I'll need your badge and keys as well."

"Okay. Let's get on with it."

Bill held his hand out to shake Jack's hand. Jack stared at Bill's hand, shook his head, then he turned around and headed for the door.

Jack had been a loyal employee who worked hard, contributed to the company's success, planned on retiring from the company in the next ten years. That all changed in an instant. He was being eliminated, not for performance, but to save expenses. Bill wasn't taking a cut in pay. Oh, he'd have to work some extra hours for a while, but he would find someone to promote at less than what Jack was making.

As Beth spoke, Jack was in a fog. He could hear her voice but couldn't listen. *What just happened? Are you kidding me?* Jack was given one week of severance for each year he was with the company—ten weeks, two and a half months of severance for ten years of his life. Beth escorted him out of the building. All of a sudden, he felt dizzy and the floor below seemed like it was moving. *Am I going to pass out?*

A light rain, almost a mist, had started to fall from the overcast sky. Thankfully, he made it to his car.

As he sat there, he watched the rain collect on his windshield. The mist became small raindrops merging with others to become larger drops. The drops began their trek down the windshield making rivulets. Jack watched the rain collect and then course down the glass. He had no idea how long he had been sitting there. The parking lot was nearly empty, and the lights had come on as the sky turned from light gray to darker gray. He glanced over to the passenger side of his Chevy Traverse. On the seat, all in one box, was his work history. Ten years of his life reduced to a Bankers Box of personal items: a few photos, business cards from customers collected over the years, a bottle of Gaviscon that he routinely ate like candy to relieve his stress-related heartburn. Also in the box were a few plaques: awards for sales performance and recognition of his membership in the Pinnacle Club, reserved only for the top performers in the company.

Jack had been a loyal employee of Wagner Enterprises for ten years beginning his career as a Regional Sales Manager. He wasn't a job hopper. He wanted to earn a good living and spend his free time with family and friends. If he had to work overtime occasionally, that was okay, it came with the territory. He always took his laptop with him on vacation and checked in several times a day to ensure his customers could get ahold of him. He was expected to keep his customers happy and he expected his colleagues would do the same. Jack had been approached by other companies through recruiters to work for competitors, but Jack was pretty happy where he was. His hard work and dedication paid off and Jack had been promoted a few times, eventually in the role of Executive Vice President of Sales. During that time, Jack had earned some latitude in his work-life balance. His boss would approve his vacation requests without question. Jack never seemed to take all of his vacation, but when he did take vacation, he was still working. He sometimes had to make sure Kathy didn't see him logging onto his email because he would end up working a few hours when he was supposed to be spending time with the family.

As he sat staring at the box, it felt like he was wearing a vest made from sandbags. He could feel the weight in his chest and just kept staring into the parking lot. A knock on the window jarred him back.

"Jack, what's up? You okay?" It was Pete, one of the IT guys. They had a relationship where Jack could go to Pete and ask how a customer request might be turned around. Was it a small t-shirt size or an XL t-shirt size? Pete was one of those people who realized that without the sales group, there would be no new customers and the IT group would have nothing to do.

"I'm fine," Jack said. "Guess I kind of spaced out."

Pete stared at the Bankers Box on the front seat. "Are you leaving? What happened? Where are you going?"

Jack sighed and glanced at the passenger seat. Everything from his office was in the front seat except for a couple of pictures that had been on the wall in his office and were now wedged between the front and rear seat. "Yeah. My job was eliminated today. Not sure where I'll go from here."

Pete's eyes widened, and his mouth fell open. "Are you serious? Who's going to lead sales?"

"I'm not sure, Pete, probably Bill until he figures something out unless he already had a plan that he didn't share with me."

"Will you go to a competitor?" Pete asked.

"Not likely. I have a non-compete agreement, and I don't see a competitor wanting to deal with that, so it limits my options for at least a year."

"That's crap," said Pete. "How can they enforce that when they eliminated your job?"

"It doesn't really stipulate how or why the separation occurs. Whether it is voluntary or involuntary, the non-compete is still in force. Guess I never thought it would affect me."

"Jack, I have to get home but let's get together. I want to know what I can do to help. You've been a great friend to me."

"Thanks, Pete. We'll stay in touch. I'll let you know where I land."

Pete's shock made Jack wonder why he had put in so many hours. What had he gained?

Not too long ago, he dreamt of retirement from Wagner, how he and Kathy would spend more time together and maybe travel. They talked about renting a place during the summer, so the kids and grandkids would have a place to go without too much expense. Simple dreams of enjoying the fruits of his labors and all the time he had spent away from Kathy and the kids. Now that seemed like an unattainable dream. Jack's outlook seemed like the weather outside: dark and gloomy.

Sitting there in the parking lot, his mind wandered. Almost everyone was gone for the weekend. No chance to say goodbye to co-workers. He wouldn't have a chance to talk with his sales team. No telling what they will think.

He could barely think, let alone, breathe.

Now what? What would he tell Kathy? His kids? It would have almost been easier if he *had* stolen something, embezzled funds, lied to a customer, something. But none of that happened. This wasn't about performance; this was about eliminating expense. No recognition for ten years of loyal service. Jack thought back to just a few months ago when he received his ten-year service award. Bill personally thanked him for his contributions and touted his accomplishments in front of the whole company at the awards ceremony.

He pulled up to his home but couldn't remember the drive. He'd done this drive hundreds of times, thousands, but this time was different. *What's going to happen?* How would he pay his mortgage? What about the college tuition he was still paying on for his two kids? Car payments, food, it goes on and on. Will he lose the house? Where can he save? Cancel the cable TV, the Internet, sell one of the cars. His mind was filled with all the negative consequences, and he was convinced that all the bad things he had dreamed up would happen.

Usually, he would be looking forward to the weekend, time with Kathy and the kids, friends, neighbors, something is usually going on. This Friday was different. Jack's focus was not on the upcoming weekend, but what would happen come Monday.

Jack's mind was racing and not in a productive way. He was given the bum's rush after ten years of loyal, productive service. For the first time in his life, he felt like a failure. He felt alone, demoralized. Were his performance reviews and awards justified? What if the performance reviews were to make him feel good and his performance wasn't that good? What did he do wrong? What would he do now?

shock

Jack carried the box into the house and headed straight for the bedroom. He placed the box on the floor and sat on the edge of the bed, his head still in a fog. He stared at the box and thought about the last ten years. The good times were what came to mind: the Christmas Party at Bill's house when they played Pictionary; the service award he received for five years, then for ten years, how his raise a few years ago had helped to pay for Matt's wedding. The fog thickened, and it all seemed like a nightmare. He'd never been fired before. He found it hard to catch his breath. He felt numb.

The first phase of elimination is shock; it is impossible for your mind to grasp that you have been eliminated. You want to say fired but that indicates you did something wrong. It's easier to say eliminated because it is a euphemism for being fired. Whatever the terminology, you're gone and the company has already moved on. Shock is really a numbness, not anxiety (that comes later) nor anger (that comes later too.) It's like a mild concussion. You still walk through the motions but you are not sure why you are doing something. You are functioning but not reasoning and not purposeful, just walking through the motions.

Jack stood up and made his way to the living room, sat down in his chair, and clicked on the news. The news was almost a pleasant departure from the shock; it worked well as a distraction.

"So, how was your day?" Kathy's voice pierced through the fog.

"What?" Jack stared at his wife.

"I said, how was your day?"

He hesitated. If he didn't say it, maybe it wasn't true. "Not so good. My job was eliminated."

"What? What did you say? What do you mean your job was eliminated?"

"I mean that I was let go today. Bill called me in and said the company wasn't meeting their goals and they had to make some cuts, and I was one of those cuts."

"I don't understand. Who's going to manage Sales?"

"I guess Bill will manage it. He's not hiring someone else. He's looking to cut payroll expense."

"But you just had an excellent review and he said great things about you on your ten-year anniversary. How could this happen?"

"He said it wasn't personal. I'm one of the highly-compensated employees and eliminating my position is how you save money," he said without emotion.

"You seem to be taking this well."

He shook his head. "Actually, I'm not. I'm still wrestling with this. It was such a blindside that I can't believe it happened."

"So what's next? Did they give you a severance? What about insurance? Is there any outplacement service?"

"It's in the paperwork they gave me. When Beth started talking about severance and PTO and COBRA, I wasn't really listening. I was thinking, *What do I do now? Where will I go?* "

Jack, the typically fun-loving, outgoing dad, sunk deeper into his chair, the weight of the job loss heavy on his mind. He couldn't feel much right now.

Jack ate dinner without saying a word. He kept thinking about what's next, and on Monday, he had nowhere to go.

Kathy had also been quiet. She seemed to have skipped the shock and anxiety and went straight to anger. "How could they do this?" she asked, her voice curt. "You've been a loyal employee and contributed to their success. Why *you*?"

Jack is feeling like everyone in his position feels. Why was I the target? The shock of being eliminated is still directing his thoughts and actions. Jack wants to feel like he'll be okay, but he has heard stories of other friends or acquaintances that were not okay. His mind will focus on the negatives and while he is still in shock, it will be hard to convince him otherwise.

Later on in the evening, the shock remained, but at least he didn't have to deal with it for a couple of days. What would he say when someone asked, "How's work?" Would he say, "I was let go," or "I was downsized," or "I was blindsided"? He didn't want to say he was fired but he couldn't help feeling like that. Jack knew it wasn't performance related but, if it wasn't, then why was *he* selected? What made *him* a target? If there were cutbacks, sales should be the *last* to go. Maybe Bill thought the sales leader position was less crucial and anyone could do it, even him.

Jack returned to his chair and flipped on the TV. He didn't want to talk. Kathy asked a million questions: who else was let go; was his boss taking a pay cut; what was severance package; how can Bill do the sales leader job? All good questions but Jack couldn't think very clearly right now.

He wasn't sure what had happened, and he was searching for rationale, for something to make sense of this. He felt like a deer in the headlights.

Jack tried to focus on the TV program, but it wasn't working. He felt sick. His stomach hurt. He had a throbbing headache. The weight of the shock made him feel like that sandbag vest was replaced by lead. After a couple of hours, he was mentally exhausted, so he went to the bedroom, his footsteps heavy and burdened.

Jack fell asleep easily. When he woke up, he was surprised that he had not been tossing and turning. It seemed like he'd been asleep all night. He sat up to peer at the clock across the room. He'd been asleep for two hours. *Now what?* He was fully awake, and his mind was racing again. The shock has begun to wear off and the reality of the elimination had set in. Fear and anxiety crept in. He couldn't sleep. He got up and gathered the paperwork he was given. He read through the severance package and realized that it would last a few months.

He logged onto to their online banking account to study the bank balances. Lots of bills and not much in savings, maybe enough for a few months after the severance runs out. Where could they save? What was his plan? They probably had six to eight months before they ran out of money. What expenses could they reduce or eliminate? He thought about small, immediate savings that were easy and in total might extend their savings a month or two. Surely, he would have a job before that.

He made a list to discuss with Kathy. They needed to make cuts immediately.

anxiety

Jack hadn't cried since his dad died several years ago. He didn't think he would have an emotional reaction to a job elimination. The emotions took over without warning and he couldn't stop them. The attack passed and he settled down somewhat. It was still dark outside and the rain had stopped. He sat in his home office staring out the window at the stillness of the night. Nothing moved, no wind, no animals, and no neighbors. The street was deserted. He felt so alone.

Jack is focusing on the negative. It's natural. Having never been in this situation, not having looked for a job in ten years and now suddenly thrust into this, he is panicking. He sits there in the quiet of the house in the middle of the night and the anxiety takes over. A panic attack comes at him without warning. He's never had a panic attack and so doesn't know what to expect. His body is covered in a cold sweat. His heart rate is elevated. His emotions are out of control and he puts his head down and begins to cry. He can't stop it. He is not in control. He doesn't want anyone to see him like this. They will think he has lost it. He's been out of work for less than a day and he's already feeling like this. What happens if this goes on for weeks or months? The downward spiral has begun.

He wondered if he could still get some sleep. He could go down to the family room and relax in his chair. Or he could climb back into bed.

If he fell asleep in the chair and Kathy found him in the morning, she'd worry. He's never had a problem sleeping. He went back to bed. He stared at the ceiling fan as it turned, pushing the air downward. He tried to think positive thoughts, but the negative thoughts were easier to rationalize. He dozed but his mind continued to focus on the negatives. He had no plan. How would he go about finding a new job? He was too young to retire, and he had to compete with people who were half his age and would work for half as much. He was a mess. Hours later, Jack finally drifted off to sleep.

Bright light sliced through the room and dust particles floated in the sunlight. Jack remembered when he was a little boy, watching the same scene play out in front of him. Sunlight shining through the Venetian blinds in his room, cutting across his bed with the dust particles floating aimlessly in the bright sun. How simple those times were. Nothing to worry about except what games would the gang play that day and who would be outside. It seemed to be the same group every day but that didn't matter.

Then he thought about his dad and how he had also been let go from his job. At the time, Jack didn't realize what was going on. His dad never graduated high school, barely made it through grade school, joined the military to support his mother and sisters, and eventually went off to war. When he came home, he was short on skills and didn't have the education to get a "big" job. Less than a year after losing his job, he suffered a stroke that left him disabled. Jack's dad was only 54 years old. Did the job loss trigger the stroke? Was the stress too much? Jack was confident that his dad never discussed what he was going through with anyone. *Suck it up and move on.*

As he stared at the sunlight creeping across the floor, he wondered, *was it a dream?* More like a nightmare, really. As he snapped back to the present, he knew that it wasn't a dream. The Bankers Box sat on the floor of the bedroom under the window. It had happened. His job was eliminated. *Now what?* He didn't want to think about it. There would be many distractions today with errands to run, chores to do around the house, and he and Kathy had dinner plans. He started to think about what he could do.

Jack was now thinking rationally, and he was confident he could find something quickly. His skills and talents were highly transferable, and he had a great track record for success as a salesperson and a sales leader.

Kathy wanted to talk about the situation, but Jack really didn't want to talk about it because he didn't have any answers. He had always been a person with a plan. He always knew what to do next. His positive attitude had always worked for them. Whether it was buying their first house or paying for schools, he always knew they could work it out. He wanted this to be the same. But he was totally unprepared for this job elimination, and a lot of things were now working against him.

There was a stigma about being eliminated. He felt the shame of a job loss, and the positive attitude he's had for so many years was gone. In its place was anxiety. Kathy didn't have the same anxiety. She shared that she wanted Bill Wagner to know what he'd done to Jack and take responsibility. She didn't want him to get off so easy by chalking it up to "that's business."

Jack could only hear every third word Kathy was saying. He heard responsibility, business. Business was made up of people. The employee-employer relationship was never equilateral. When an employee left the company, the workload was reassigned, or a replacement person was hired. No harm, no foul. When the company terminated an employee, that employee's financial and emotional foundations were destroyed.

"So, what's the plan? Will you will stay in the industry or try to find something else?" Kathy asked.

"I'm not sure. I have a non-compete, but I don't know how that works if terminated. I don't even know how our competitors would look at this. Will they think I did something wrong?"

"Well, I can go back to work," Kathy offered. "I know it's not much, but it would be something."

"Let's hope that I can find a job quickly and then you wouldn't have to go back to work. I know how much you value your free time and you'd have to quit your volunteer work. Let's wait a couple of weeks and see what happens. I read through the severance package, and I'll get almost four months of full pay with my vacation, PTO, and severance, and we have some savings, so we have a bit of time."

"We should at least prepare, just in case, right?"

"Sure, but the first thing we need to do is look at our expenses. Where can we save money? We should sit down and go through the 'must-haves' from the 'nice-to-haves.'"

Jack had already glanced at some of this last night when he couldn't sleep.

"I think we should consider refinancing the house," said Jack. "We're on a 15-year mortgage plan. We might look at moving that back to a 30-year mortgage and reduce our monthly payments. It resets the clock on our mortgage, but it definitely reduces the monthly expense and that's our largest expense every month."

"Do we know what we currently spend every month and if we made these cuts, what's the minimum we need to meet our bills?" asked Kathy.

Jack hadn't done that math. They had never really lived on a budget and as long as they could meet their expenses, they were okay. The negative thoughts and anxiety were just below the surface and his emotions were fragile, but he didn't want Kathy to know that. Jack had always been the breadwinner. He'd always been the one to tell the family not to worry, "I got this." Now, he wasn't so sure.

"I've never done a budget for us. We've always had enough to do what we wanted. I know about what we spend every month and we were putting money into our 401(k) and contributing to our savings. I need to sit down and figure out where we can really save and how much we need to live on, so I know the minimum salary I can accept."

Jack had been in tactical mode, just relating facts. The anxiety had been pushed down, and he'd just been working with facts, not really considering options.

Kathy's voice interrupted his thoughts. "What about our 401(k)? Can we tap into that? How much do we have there? I know you were thinking about refinancing, but what if we sold the house and downsized? The kids are gone, and we don't need a big house."

"Whoa, whoa, whoa! This is Day One. Let's not overreact. Let me come up with a plan before we start making radical changes. We need to have some contingencies, but what if I find a job right away? I've always had a job and my skills are pretty transferable. I don't think I'll have a problem."

Jack started to feel more positive. Sure, he was blindsided, but he was now gaining his confidence back. He *could* make this work. He'd been successful in sales management, no reason he couldn't do it again.

The weather outside had changed for the better and so had Jack's outlook. The gloominess from yesterday was gone, and Jack's initial reaction to the blindside had lifted. Things *would* work out.

Saturday night would be a distraction. They had dinner plans with friends, Tim and Rachel. Jack has known Tim for years and their kids went to school together. The dinner plans were made weeks ago, and Jack was looking forward to it.

Suddenly, Jack thought about the cost. Normally they would not have worried about the cost of a dinner. Now he was thinking about every expense. Could they go somewhere less expensive? Could they order something they both could share? Should he eat something before dinner and then order something small? Jack realized he was probably overcompensating, all ridiculous options, but that's what was in his mind. He felt guilty going out for dinner when he had no income. Forget about the severance and savings. They should be conserving right now and not spending money on entertainment.

And what would he say when Tim asked, "How's work going?" Should he change the subject or just blurt out that his job had been eliminated? Kathy asked if he wanted to cancel but he knew she really wanted to go. Jack decided to keep their plans just to prove that his job loss was something he could manage through, and he was already making headway. He would be fine. He would look back on this night and see how stupid he was for even thinking about canceling.

They arrived at the restaurant and Jack really didn't want to be here. However, he needed to stick it out, but he was worried. He still hadn't figured out what to say to Tim.

"Hey, Jack how's it going?" Tim asked as they enter the restaurant.

"Great. Have you been waiting long?"

"Nope, Rachel and I just got here. They should have our table in a few minutes. I called ahead and made a reservation. Do you girls want something from the bar?"

"No, I can wait until we get a table," Kathy said casually, but they were both relieved to hear the waitress calling them.

"Daniels, party of four."

"Here we are," said Tim, and the hostess escorted them to their table.

If the subject of the job came up – and there was no reason to think it wouldn't – he'd just have to be honest with Tim and tell him what happened.

"So how's work going, Jack? Our business has been off, but I hope it rebounds."

There was a pause as Jack felt the lump in his throat and his heart started to race. He took a deep breath. "Well, our business isn't doing well either, so Bill had to make some tough decisions. My job was one of the eliminations that happened yesterday," Jack explained.

And there it was, out in the open. He heard the words as he was saying them, and it seemed so matter-of-fact. Jack felt relieved about saying it out loud like it was no big deal.

"What? Are you kidding me?"

"I wish. I didn't see it coming, and it caught me by surprise. I'm sure we'll be okay. My sales management skills are pretty transferable to other companies."

"What a jackass! Bill called you in and with no warning, just let you go?"

"Yep, that's pretty much how it went. I've never had that happen before and after ten good years, I thought this might be the last chapter of my career. Guess there's another chapter I wasn't counting on."

"So what are you going to do? Do you have any prospects?"

"Not yet," Jack admitted. "It's still pretty fresh. I'm still trying to figure out what happened and haven't given any thought to what's next."

"Will you stay in the industry or try something new?"

"Staying in the industry will be a challenge since I have a non-compete for a year. If I were a sales guy, it might be easier because I'd have a definitive set of clients but being the sales leader, I touched every account that Wagner has."

"That sucks," said Tim. "I guess we all sign those non-compete agreements and never think that they'll be used. I can't believe it."

"I have some contacts that I'm going to reach out to. Hopefully, they can introduce me to people looking for someone with my skill set."

"Let me know if I can help," Tim offered.

Uncomfortable with the attention, Jack moved the conversation on to something else. Maybe Tim and Rachel were feeling sorry for him.

On the way home, Jack said, "Well, that wasn't too bad. I wasn't really sure what to say when someone asks how work is going. I thought I should just be honest and tell them that my job was eliminated."

"I think it's different with Tim and Rachel. They've known us for a long time. I don't see them as being judgmental. It might be different with other people," Kathy responded.

"You don't think they're wondering what really happened? Tim has never looked for a job. He's never been out of work. He may not have ever thought about what happens when someone's job is eliminated."

"Do you think Tim will be able to help?"

"I doubt it. It's hard for someone that knows you personally and not professionally to recommend you to someone else. It would be different if Tim and I had worked together for years, but we haven't."

"Maybe Tim knows someone that you could connect with, just an introduction."

"That's a thought. I definitely need to consider my connections and expand my network. I haven't concentrated on that in the past several years. I guess I was too busy working."

Jack had a great night's sleep and woke up refreshed on Sunday morning. As he was getting ready for church, he thought about possibilities. He knew some recruiters that he had spoken to in the past when he wasn't interested in leaving Wagner, and he had some associates that he had worked with who left Wagner and went to another industry, avoiding the non-compete issue.

Jack was feeling pretty good. Besides, there was really no expectation on Sunday; everyone was off work so Jack felt normal. He felt better about his plan and what he had to do to get out in the workforce again. This transition could be a great thing as he started to reflect back on the last few years with Wagner.

great expectations

In Daniel Pink's provocative and persuasive book, Drive, he asserts that the secret to high performance and satisfaction—at work, at school, and at home—is the deeply human need to direct our own lives, to learn and create new things, and to do better by ourselves and our world. Motivation is intrinsic and not driven exclusively by external rewards.

By Monday morning. Jack has had a couple of good nights' sleep and he was ready. Jack started by creating a list of LinkedIn connections, Facebook friends, Outlook contacts and the business cards he has accumulated over the years. He culled through the list and put aside the out-of-town contacts. Relocation wasn't an option at this point.

Jack experimented with his "elevator speech" to indicate what he was looking for and why he was looking. He needed consistency and transparency.

"Hey, Jim, this is Jack Thompson. Did I catch you at a bad time? I wanted to let you know that I'm no longer with Wagner Enterprises and I wondered if we could get together just so I could pick your brain about what you see in the market."

Would that work? What *did* Jack want? He wanted a job but unless he knew someone who was hiring, he was going to need another approach. What he wanted was to talk to people, network with people. Get perspective that he didn't have.

What about voicemail? What was the message he wanted to leave that would get someone to call him back? What about email? Was there something compelling he could use that would guarantee a response?

Jack had to approach this like he was prospecting because he *was* selling himself and this could be the hardest job he'd ever had. What were the lessons learned that he used with his sales group?

Jack reflected on his value, all the features and benefits of the "Jack Thompson" product. This would help him explain what he could bring to a company.

By the end of the day, he'd made real progress in creating his plan, but hadn't yet started "doing" anything.

Kathy popped into his home office. "So, how did it go today? Did you apply for any jobs? Did you talk to anyone who might be hiring?"

"No. I, uh, worked on updating my resume, my LinkedIn profile, and I put together my contact list and worked on getting my sales pitch down. I think I am prepared to get after it."

"That's all you got done today?"

"Well, yeah. I needed some kind of plan versus just shooting out resumes and filling out applications. I've got to have something to say when, and if, I do get someone on the phone."

"Okay. That makes sense. I just thought you would've submitted resumes for open positions," said Kathy.

Shoulders slumping, Jack went from feeling focused and productive to feeling like he hadn't accomplished anything. Kathy obviously had higher expectations of what success should've looked like.

The next day, Jack put his plan in motion. He had his email list and telephone follow-ups to get meetings. Jack wasn't looking for a job – not yet – he wanted meetings. If he just asked for meetings to discuss the market, expand his network, find out more about a specific industry, then he'd be more successful at getting in front of people.

Their defenses would come down because they didn't have to worry about having to say they weren't hiring.

The plan worked, and Jack scheduled several meetings in the next week.

"Have you gone to the unemployment office yet?" Kathy asked.

"I don't think I'll need to. I'll have something pretty quick. I have meetings scheduled for next week and will hopefully have some for the following week."

Jack continued to work his plan, and for the first two weeks, he was confident that he would land a job fairly quickly. He kept a positive attitude with Kathy, but he was still talking to himself, and there were doubts.

"Do you think we need to make some changes?" Kathy asked him. "It's been a couple of weeks, and we should talk about it."

"We'll be okay," assured Jack. "I've been making a lot of connections and still think something will happen soon."

"Shouldn't we have a timeline? Something that says if you don't have a new job by this date that we need to make changes?"

"You're right," Jack conceded.

"So, let's talk about what changes we will need to make. I'm not sure that the small changes we've made will make any real impact. We need to look at some significant lifestyle changes. Maybe sell the house. What about unemployment and our 401(k)? I know you didn't want to talk about this, but perhaps we should now."

BOOM! His chest tightened and his stomach churned. Another panic attack. Kathy had never been one to ignore the "elephant in the room." Unemployment? That was a blow to his ego. Unemployment followed by selling the house for something smaller? Blow number two. Success was often measured by possessions, and Jack didn't like being challenged to give up a possession and take on a smaller one, which made him feel like everything he had worked for meant nothing.

Jack couldn't remember if Kathy had ever seen him break down. Maybe at the funeral for his sister or his dad, but not just for "no reason." Jack had never been an emotional person, but now he couldn't control it. He had to release it. His eyes teared and he began to shake. He knew that Kathy loved him, but he didn't want to expose his vulnerability to her.

"I'm sorry, Jack. I know you're going through a lot right now. It's going to be all right." She kissed his cheek and quietly exited the room.

Jack thought about a friend who lost his job a couple years ago. Mike had been blindsided, as well, and while Jack felt sorry for him and wanted to help, he really didn't know how. What he didn't know about Mike, and found out later, was that Mike had become so depressed by the job loss that he had considered suicide.

Mike left the house early one morning and drove to a secluded spot not far from their house, somewhere where his family wouldn't be the ones to find him. In the backseat was a loaded 12-gauge shotgun, and he intended to use it. Mike wanted the panic attacks to stop. He couldn't control his emotions, and he couldn't think of a solution, so he decided the best solution was to end his life. He parked his car in a secluded spot, pulled the gun from the backseat and with tears streaming down his face, he put the shotgun in his mouth and pulled the trigger. It didn't go off. He sat there wondering what had happened. The hand of God had saved him, and his thoughts went not to his pain but to the pain he would've inflicted on his family if he had succeeded. He hadn't considered that before and as these thoughts rushed forward, he decided *not* to end his life but to surrender to God and to His will. Mike *would* find work again. It may not be what he wanted but it would be what he needed. His lifestyle may need to change but that was okay.

At the time, Jack hadn't realized how much pain Mike had been in. He couldn't understand how a person could lose his job. Now he understood. He felt out of control. He felt desperate. His ego was bruised, and his pride, destroyed. He worried about what would happen and more importantly, what people would think. He exposed his shallowness and how he valued the possessions he had accumulated as a sign of his success.

As the head-of-household, the breadwinner, he was challenged that perhaps he was not as good as he thought. More responsibility brought with it more chances for failures and less time to chart new directions. If he hadn't had the same responsibilities as the head-of-household, he may not have understood what was happening. He wouldn't have seen the destruction of the ego and the impact that had. He hadn't understood that some suggestions or comments that he may have made casually before could have made the situation worse for someone battling the job loss, by identifying actions that could contribute to that deflated ego.

Jack hadn't gotten much sleep the night before, but he was hoping it was just an odd occurrence. He hadn't realized that this would become the "new normal," sleepless nights followed by anxious days, looking forward to the weekends when he could be normal like everyone else. Jack's "new normal" was to fall asleep quickly, and, within a few hours, be wide awake. He'd already been over the bills and finances. He couldn't keep doing that in the middle of the night. He began a new routine of heading downstairs and turning on the TV. For a while he was able to place his focus elsewhere. He watched mindless TV programs and didn't have to think too much. After a couple of hours, he fell back to sleep with the TV on, remaining in the chair in the family room.

Most mornings, he would awaken but not feel refreshed. Falling back to sleep and waking again. He just wanted this anxiety to go away.

For the last ten years, he had driven to the office. The more he thought about how his life had changed so dramatically in such a short period of time, the more he became angry and the more he wanted his life to return to the way it was.

anger

What *had* happened? Why was *Jack* the one let go? Maybe he had
just gotten to a level where he knew too much and that was threatening
to someone. Maybe his salary had increased to a level that was too
high and rather than have a discussion about a salary reduction, it was
easier to eliminate his job. They hadn't even appeared to search for an
alternative position for him, if it truly *was* a job elimination. Ten years
of solid service meant nothing.

He had more loyalty to the company than the company had to him.
He slammed his fist onto his desk. Jack wanted his boss to feel the
same pain he was feeling. He wanted their business to fail. He wanted
retribution. Jack put his job search on hold and searched the Internet
for information on age discrimination and illegal termination. Now he
thought about suing Wagner.

What Jack found out is that age discrimination was nearly
impossible to prove. Unless someone outwardly told him that he was
too old, and they were going to hire someone younger, he was not
going to be able to make a case for age discrimination. He also
discovered what an "employee-at-will" means. He may have read that
in the Employee Handbook but had never really thought the term
pertained to him. He realized that when a company wanted to
terminate someone, they could do so without cause at any time. The
easiest way was job elimination, which came down to a Reduction-In-
Force or RIF. Such actions did not reflect the way Jack was raised or
the way he would want to treat people.

After hours researching age discrimination, he realized he had
wasted time chasing a plan that would likely lead nowhere instead of

sticking with his original plan to find a job, but the anger had taken over.

Jack avoided the searches on job boards. They all had the same postings. LinkedIn included a few that were different. There definitely was some "head trash" when it came to job postings. He'd heard that no one gets hired from those postings. Most of those jobs were filled before the posting happened. Perhaps this was all busy work and not really productive in moving him closer to his next job. He needed to focus on getting his resume in front of more hiring managers.

In the ensuing weeks, Jack attended a couple of networking events. These were designed to assist people who were "in transition." Guess what? Everyone who attended these events was out of work. If Jack felt positive when he walked in, he certainly didn't feel that way when he left. While he picked up some pointers and tactical approaches to job search, he also picked up some negatives from other people in transition. He heard how some people have been out of work for many months with no imminent prospects. He heard how people his age were being passed over for younger people who would work for less and that companies didn't put the same value on experience and maturity they once did. He heard how the interview processes had changed with assessment tests prior to even a telephone screening call, and he hadn't taken an assessment test since he applied to college. He wasn't feeling so good. He shouldn't have gone to those events.

The bottom line: he learned that networking worked but networking with other out-of-work people may not be THE networking that was most productive.

Jack doubled his efforts on his own network and reached out to make new connections. That's how he would find his next opportunity. He considered working for a competitor just to get back at his former company. The anger and bitterness remained, but he was trying to channel it to a positive outcome. He considered taking an entry-level job with a competitor only to take advantage of his knowledge base. He wouldn't do anything to violate his non-compete or his confidentiality agreement, but he wanted to find a way to inflict pain on his former company. He was only thinking of his boss now, not his friends who were still there. He wanted Bill to experience what he was feeling.

"Did you go to the Unemployment Office?" Kathy asked.

"No. I guess I should have gone there this morning. I started working on the job search and completely forgot about it. I'll go tomorrow."

Jack had been employed for almost 40 years and never collected a dime of assistance. Maybe now *was* the time. The extra money would help them pay the mortgage payment. While Jack knew this was only temporary, he couldn't help feeling like a failure; like something didn't go right, so he had to collect unemployment benefits.

Despite his feelings, Jack's mind was made up; he would file for unemployment benefits tomorrow. No one needed to know. He went online to see if he could just fill out the required paperwork without going to an office. No such luck. As a first-time filer, he would have to visit the office and complete the paperwork.

He arrived at the office the next day. It was a claustrophobic room with too many chairs and too many privacy dividers. He took a number and waited. There were a lot of people here: some talking to staff members, others filling out paperwork, some searching the database and some applying for jobs. Even with all the activity, he felt like everyone was staring at him. What if he ran into someone he knew? Why did he feel so bad about taking advantage of assistance that he'd contributed to for almost 40 years?

"Number 37," a woman's voice called.

"Yes, that's me," replied Jack. He followed the girl to her desk.

"Hi, I'm Sandra Brown, and I'm a Career Counselor with the Department of Labor for the state." The girl was young, wore too much makeup and talked too quickly. She held out her hand. "So, how are you, Mr..."

"Thompson, Jack." He shook her hand. "I've been better. I've never applied for unemployment benefits before."

"No worries," Sandra assured him. "The process is very simple. I'm here to help you in the transition. There are several forms for you to fill out to apply and some guidelines for what you need to do to continue to receive benefits."

"Okay. Can I take the forms home and fill them out?"

"No, when we finish here, you can go online with your personal login and complete the forms here before you leave today. First, let's review your background and experience so I can assist you in the job search. You have an impressive resume. Your last position was Executive Vice President of Sales. Few people come through here who even have a resume; most of the people are looking for hourly employment."

Another jab that Sandra wasn't even aware she delivered. *Really?* Jack had swallowed his pride to come here only to be told that most people in management positions didn't apply for assistance. Why not?

Were they too embarrassed? Did they get jobs right away? Did they have so much saved or investments that they didn't need the help? Coming here was a bad idea.

"Sandra, how long have you been a Career Counselor here?" Jack asked.

"Well, about four months."

"What did you do before that?"

"In college. I majored in Social Work. This is my first job after graduation."

Awesome. Jack was discussing his career with someone who could be one of his kids. She was probably good at what she did, but she had no experience with upper-management positions.

"Once you complete the application, you'll need to keep a log of applications you submit. We have a tracking form, or you can use your own, as long as you track them. You must apply for three jobs every week to maintain your benefits."

"Three?"

"Yes, at least three per week to maintain your benefits. Your benefits have a maximum of 20 weeks, and we will have to meet face-to-face once a month."

"Great. Do we set up that next meeting now?"

"Yes. Let's get you set up on the computer so you can log in to the Unemployment Benefits portal and complete the application. Then, before you leave, we'll make sure you completed everything, then make an appointment for our follow-up meeting."

Sandra accompanied Jack to one of the computers against the wall and showed him how to log on to the Unemployment Benefits portal.

She pointed out the tutorial on how to navigate the website and how to look for job openings. This was more humiliating than he had imagined. This wasn't a good idea. There were probably people who needed the benefits more than he does. Why was he here? He'd had enough. He wanted to leave.

He forced himself to complete the application and to search for job openings that matched his experience, skill and employment level – nothing. He scheduled his next meeting with Sandra and headed out the door to his car.

Jack sat in his car, banged the dashboard and screamed. He tried to rationalize how having his pride destroyed was worth the extra income. He was learning humility at light speed, and it was no fun. The "system" was set up to humiliate people at a time when they already felt like a failure.

How could anyone find a job when they only applied for three per week? Jack should be applying for three per day! The log that he had to keep might not even be reviewed. *What?* If this was really counseling, wouldn't they want to see where the applications were being made? Make some recommendations if he was not getting to the next step? Direct him to websites with interview preparation questions, sample assessment tests, and resume tips to get past the screener? Something!

anxiety ii

With the humiliation of the unemployment process behind him, Jack started the next day with redoubled efforts. His routine thus far hadn't been what he was used to and that needed to change. Dealing with the initial shock, then anxiety and anger, Jack decided to create a serious plan and stick to it.

His new plan was to attack this job search just like he would if he were in sales and needed to close some business. Finding a job *became* his new job. His new routine was to get up, shower, shave and get dressed like he was going to work; no shorts, sweats, t-shirts. He needed to feel the part and that meant taking this seriously. If he happened to get a spur-of-the-moment meeting, he wanted to be ready.

The plan was to use Mondays as his research day. He'd search positions on the job boards, research companies that were in a growth mode and then look for connections that he may have to someone at those companies. Mondays were the days he wanted to reach out with phone calls and emails to get in front of people. The expectation was that no one would respond on Monday.

Tuesdays, Wednesdays, and Thursdays were set aside for networking, the days to schedule meetings and network with connections. The networking could be a phone call, coffee at a location that worked for the other person or even lunch. Maybe it would be a meeting at their office. The objective was to have face-to-face interactions to refine his skills on interviewing in a more relaxed atmosphere without the pressure of trying to get an offer. He could always learn something from those meetings: new connections, new industries, growth companies, maybe it would just be someone who knew him and who could help him focus his skills and expertise in a few areas instead of trying to be all things to all employers.

Friday would be his planning day. This would be for follow-ups, setting meetings for the next week, making changes to his resume and updating his profile. Each day would start with a plan, blocking time for searches on job boards, company websites, LinkedIn connections that may have a new job and applying for those positions that would be a good fit for him and the company. He was ready.

He also needed to ensure that his attitude was correct. Deep down, he just wanted a job. He wanted to feel useful because right now, he didn't feel useful. That feeling could project itself as desperation and that was the last thing he wanted. He tried to feel like he had won the lottery and didn't need the job. That way, his conversations would be more genuine, and he wouldn't feel desperation. In truth, Jack found the process more humiliating than he had imagined.

Jack expected his plan to yield different results but Wednesday night was just like the past few nights. Fall asleep quickly and wide awake at 3:00 AM. *This can't go on.* Jack was exhausted by dawn and wasn't getting any sleep. He had to do something.

The next day, Kathy approached Jack in his office. "Jack, I know you're getting up every night. Perhaps you should see the doctor. Maybe he can prescribe something? Or...maybe you can try an over-the-counter sleep-aid? You're starting your day exhausted."

"I'm okay. I'm sure it's just a temporary thing. I'll be fine."

"Promise me that if this continues, you'll do something. I don't want you to end up in the hospital."

"If this goes on, I'll try a sleep-aid that's over-the-counter."

When Kathy left, Jack slumped in his chair. He didn't want to go to the doctor. That would be another defeat for him. He was angry and upset but pushed all of those feelings down. Then he wouldn't have to deal with them.

On Thursday, Jack restarted with his new routine and combed through his connections. He searched for people he could meet with, those who may have a different perspective on the market, an industry or a company. He reached out first to friends he had known for some time.

What came next was *not* something he had expected. Many of his friends were busy with their own jobs and family. When he requested a casual coffee or lunch just to talk, they had other commitments. They offered to help by saying, "Let me know what I can do" or "Let me know if I can help."

He believed they would make time for him. He thought they would sit down and try to understand what he was going through and not have to ask how to help; instead, he expected they would offer to take some actions. He was wrong. Some of the people were really just acquaintances, people he had known for years but not really friends. Maybe they felt like unemployment was contagious and if they spent time with him, they could be next. Or, maybe they really did want to help but didn't know how and it was easier to steer away from it. Maybe they didn't want to risk their reputation for fear that Jack was not that good of an employee and supporting him would be a negative reflection on them.

He had a plan, his prospecting plan, but that was for reaching out to people he didn't know. He didn't think he would have a problem meeting with friends. Maybe this was all *him*. Maybe *he* was the problem. Did *he* alienate people as he was moving up the ladder? Did *he* not make time for people who had the same requests? Did *he* make judgments about people whose jobs were eliminated? Did *he* talk about other people who had been in similar situations in the past whose jobs were eliminated, and he couldn't understand how a valuable employee could be eliminated? He was listening to the voices in his head again and they told him that he had no "real" friends, just acquaintances.

He felt alone. Kathy was his support, but she couldn't understand how he was feeling right now. How could some of his long-standing friends really think this job elimination could be *his* fault? The perception *was* real.

The anxiety returned. Jack felt the need for a job stronger than ever. Not a job at the same level in title, responsibility, or pay, just a job. He considered alternatives, lower-level jobs where he could earn an hourly wage and contribute to the family support. He worried about the budget again and wanted to rerun the numbers to determine what was the least amount they could live on and how they could make that income. The anxiety of not being able to pay his current bills and now the lack of activity in finding a job was causing him to think irrationally. He fantasized about just having an hourly job with no stress – a "job," not a career. Part of him knew the anxiety would pass, but he couldn't feel that now.

Jack started to consider entry-level jobs that he knew he was overqualified for but the chances of being eliminated a second time were less. Perhaps he should think about owning his own business. What if he could find a franchise? How about consulting? He knew people who had been eliminated that had new jobs with XYZ Consulting or XYZ & Associates, and the XYZ was always **their** initials. Did he want to put in that many hours at this point in his career? What type of business would benefit from his experience and skill set? Jack's mind was all over the board. He couldn't focus because he couldn't think rationally. He wished things would go back to the way they were.

letting go

Jack wanted to stop the emotional rollercoaster, but he didn't know how. Little victories like getting a meeting were soon replaced with depression from a rejection letter. He wanted this to stop. He felt like he was on a hamster wheel, running but not going anywhere.

The lack of sleep became a bigger issue. He tried going to bed later, thinking if he was overly tired, he could get some sleep. No chance. He routinely woke up at 3:00 AM and logged onto the computer to search for new job openings. Forget about the fact that he was probably not at his peak performance in the middle of the night; at least the activity made him feel productive. After a couple of hours, he grew tired and returned to bed, but was back up in an hour.

He tried some over-the-counter sleep-aids. The sleeping pills had no effect and his routine of a few hours' sleep, followed by a couple of waking hours, followed by another hour of sleep continued. He was exhausted. It seemed like he could only sleep well on Friday and Saturday nights because he could truly "shut down" and not feel the pressure of applying for jobs, getting meetings, or attending networking events. Perhaps his subconscious knew that it was okay to take off for the weekend, but when Sunday night rolled around, he was back to the sleepless pattern.

Jack had to break this cycle so he could stay on a positive track. He had to stay focused. He thought he was making progress. The small successes didn't last long, and the negative thoughts were easier to conjure. The longer it continued, the worse it got. He wasn't sure if he should talk to a counselor or his doctor or both.

Kathy suggested talking to a counselor.

"Maybe. I haven't thought about that. I never thought I would need to. I've always just worked through things myself."

Jack was scheduled to go back to the Unemployment Office for his check-in with Sandra. Had it really been four weeks? He hated this. He was somewhat over the humiliation and the extra money *was* helping make ends meet until he found his next opportunity, but he still didn't want to go.

He showed up at the office, signed in, and waited for Sandra. After 30 minutes, they called his number and he was directed to a cubicle with a new counselor. The new counselor could've also been one of his kids, fresh out of college with a degree in Social Work, just like Sandra, and advising Jack how to find a management job. This counselor had never been out of work. She was too young to have had an experience close to this. Like Sandra, she likely had never worked in business nor been in management, so all of the advice was going to be theory from what she had learned in college. Counselors learned to teach their clients to focus on behaviors like sending out three resumes a day or checking multiple job boards.

Jack needed help with his attitude, not behaviors or techniques. He could brush up his resume or LinkedIn profile all day long and he wouldn't be any closer to a new position. And, while right now he needed help with his attitude, some of the behaviors *had* changed. The new screening process required applicants to take a variety of assessment tests, including psychological, English, math, personality, and logic. This was the new screening process BEFORE you even talked to a real person. Jack would cross this bridge when he came to it. He had to get his attitude adjusted first. Jack stared at the new counselor and she stared back.

I hate this! What are you thinking? Do you really think I haven't been to all the job boards? Do you think I haven't been working to expand my network? Do you think there is some new revelation that you offer that I haven't thought of already?

The screams and the tirade were in his head. If he had lost it right there, they probably would have escorted him off the premises. He was beyond frustrated. He was beyond humiliated. He was talking to a kid with no practical experience. But it wasn't the "kid's" fault. The system was designed to move people through the process and assumed everyone was trying to scam the system. He couldn't wait to get home.

The emotional rollercoaster was now a daily thing. Jack wanted to celebrate small successes; a meeting with someone who could provide market insight or knew someone at a company that might be looking for someone with his skills and experience; an opportunity to discuss his resume with a hiring manager; an assessment test that was step two in the process. Not big wins, just small steps that show progress.

No one really understood how those were victories. It wasn't an interview, but at least he was talking to someone and that was something. He had to find a way to let go of this process and not be stressed out by it. Jack thought he had been in control of his work life, even his family life. When he thought he was in control and things did not go according to his plan, he became frustrated or angry.

The ups and downs were emotionally wearing him out. Panic attacks hit him when he least expected. He was living on a tipping point where his spirits could be raised without much effort, but a panic attack could send him spiraling into depression. One phone call that resulted in a meeting made him feel euphoric. One email rejection letter depressed him, and he thought he would never find work again. There had to be a way to stop the cycle or at least smooth out the hills and valleys.

"'At issue here is the question – "To whom do I belong? To God, or to the world?"' Many of my daily preoccupations suggest that I belong more to the world than to God. A little criticism makes me angry, and a little rejection makes me depressed. A little praise raises my spirits, and a little success excites me. It takes very little to raise me up or thrust me down. Often I am like a small boat on the ocean completely at the mercy of its waves. All the time and energy I spend in keeping some kind of balance and preventing myself from being tipped over and drowning, shows that my life is mostly a struggle for survival: not a holy struggle, but an anxious struggle resulting from the mistaken idea that it is the world that defines me."

The Return of the Prodigal Son – Henri J. M. Nouwen

Jack remembered reading or hearing something about the four aspects to a human person: physical, emotional, intellectual, and spiritual. Maybe that's why Jack felt so out of control. Physically he was a wreck. He hadn't slept well in months. He wasn't eating well, and he had no workout routine. This aspect was definitely out of balance.

Emotionally, he had ups and downs, sideways, stomach always felt queasy. Aspect number two was also out of balance. He realized he had to give more priority to his relationships. He had been so inwardly focused that his emotions were not in control.

Intellectually, Jack had always strived to learn more, but since the job elimination, that was out the window. His intellectual experience had been relegated to networking techniques, interviewing preparation, job hunting and company research. All good things but not the kind of thing that helped you grow as a person. Aspect number three, some, but still not in balance.

Jack had never been religious. He attended church with Kathy and the kids when they were growing up, and he and Kathy still went every Sunday, but that was the extent of it. Jack had never been engaged with his faith. Jack hadn't been engaged with his faith since he was in grade school. His story wasn't much different from many of his friends: stopped going to church during his high school years with the exception of the required attendance from his parents; off to college and no one to check on him, so attendance was reduced to Christmas and Easter. Spirituality, leg number four, out of balance.

Jack had to pay more attention to getting enough sleep, eating right and doing some exercise. Hopefully, that would help him to get the sleep he had been missing.

After they got married, Kathy had been more involved in her faith than Jack. She wanted to attend church every Sunday, so Jack went along. He just never engaged. Jack prayed with the family at meals but that was it. He believed in God but just didn't have Him at the top of his priority list. Jack's priorities (if he were honest with himself) were Jack, his family, everyone else, and then – maybe – God. He might be inclined to change that order to put God ahead of everyone else, if he thought about it for a while or if he were challenged.

He had become so secularized that he had not even considered God as his support. Kathy reminded him that God was in control of this situation and that He always had been in control. Jack heard her, but her words didn't seem to sink in. He wasn't buying it. Jack needed practical advice that could get him off this rollercoaster.

God had gotten Jack's attention with the job loss, but now Jack needed to reset his priorities. Jack heard about a men's retreat taking place in a few weeks. He had never been on a retreat, but he felt like this might be something that would be good for him. Maybe the quiet time to refocus would be good. He was having difficulty doing that on his own. He felt like he was working his plan, but it wasn't happening fast enough and maybe he needed to reset his priorities. The retreat was only a couple of days. *What could it hurt?* He signed up.

Jack was apprehensive about attending and as the day of the retreat approached, he was having second thoughts. He wasn't sure why he even signed up. He felt compelled to do it but wasn't sure why. Worst case was that it would not be what he expected, and he could mysteriously leave at a break since Jack didn't know anyone who was attending and figured no one would hold him accountable.

The day arrived, and Jack went with no expectations. He thought he might listen to a couple of speakers, meet a few new people and have time for reflection. He hoped this wasn't a mistake.

The retreat began, but it was not what he expected. The speakers were not trained retreat masters; they were just regular men who had a story to tell and all of them were touched by God through the Holy Spirit. These men all had similar stories regarding how they tried to handle issues on their own; were helped by the Holy Spirit; and have since reprioritized their lives. All of them indicated they were happier today than they have ever been. Some had more difficult struggles than a job loss but were able to find peace and happiness through their focus on God.

This retreat was way outside Jack's comfort zone. He wanted to leave, and he was fearful that he was going to be asked to share his own struggles. They assured everyone that no one would be asked to share anything, but Jack was still not comfortable. The alternative was to go home, sit on the couch and worry about what would happen on Monday. Jack decided to stay and hoped for the best.

By Sunday afternoon, Jack viewed his world differently. He realized how shallow and petty he had been and how his lack of faith had put him in a place where he only believed in himself. How could a change of this magnitude happen so quickly? Jack had no expectation of any change. He thought this would be a respite from the voices in his head, not a change in his emotional and spiritual self.

The men who shared their stories with the group during those two days were no different than Jack. They had faced adversity and thought they could handle it all on their own. Their faith had been self-centered. This was an epiphany, an awakening. These men submitted their will to God and their lives had changed for the better.

Jack felt ashamed for having been so self-centered to think that only he mattered, and he felt happiness through understanding that he was not alone in his struggles. Finally, Jack had a realization that this change signified more than just hope.

He realized what Kathy meant when she said he was not in control and never has been. Jack realized his priorities needed to change. If he put God first, others second (including his family), and himself third, he would have a new perspective, one that was not centered on *him*.

What *was* he really seeking? Jack knew what it was: that long-lasting happiness that was almost unshakeable, that happiness where everyone wanted to live their lives.

When he arrived home, Kathy asked how it went.

"Really well. I have a better understanding of what true happiness looks like. I had some time to think about the things that I spend time on; what makes me happy and what makes me angry. It gave me a chance to really ask 'who cares.' Even simple stuff like someone cutting me off on the highway. Does it make me feel better to yell at them; honk the horn or something worse? Maybe temporarily but how important is it not to let them get in front of me? Will I save five minutes? I need to quit judging other people; it's not my job."

Kathy asked, "Wow. You learned all that in two days at a retreat?"

"Yes." Jack was definitely more at peace after this retreat and he realized how the job search and his focus to make a contribution had added too much stress into his life.

Jack was uneasy with some of these revelations, but he now had more clarity and was less anxious. The desperation of finding a job had subsided. His role was to put in the hard work of finding a job and let God decide when and where his next opportunity would arise. Jack didn't have to force the situation. He couldn't believe that two days at a retreat could do for him what counseling could not. He must let go: let go of the desperation, let go of the feelings of failure, let go of thinking he can fix this by himself, let go of keeping to himself and not talking to Kathy about what he was feeling. He must let go of asking "Why me?"

anxiety iii

Jack was a new person on Monday. He was more focused, and he approached the job search with a new perspective. No more applying to positions that weren't a good fit. His next opportunity must be a good fit for him and for the company. Although he has worn many hats in the past, only one had really made him feel like he was using his talents to the fullest. Now he needed to concentrate on that. He needed to find companies that lacked what he offered and network with people that might be aware of companies looking for his skill set.

He started his day with prayer. Not the same rote prayers he learned as a child but a real conversation. He wouldn't be going over the list of things he wanted but instead started with gratitude for what he had: his family, his health, and the talents he has been given. His attitude was different, and he felt it.

With his newfound focus, Jack was off to the races. He culled through opportunities on the job boards; researched growth companies in the area and reached out to his network of friends and colleagues to get meetings – not asking for a job, repeating his plan of meeting with people and finding out what the market looked like from their perspective.   Jack's efforts started to pay off and he was getting interest from companies where he had applied. He didn't expect to find any opportunities on the job boards. But he *was* getting some traction. The companies wanted him to complete the first of many online assessments before he had an opportunity for a face-to-face interview.

It used to be that you tried to find a connection at the company with the job posting. They might be able to inform you of the process; know the hiring manager; recommend you for the position; anything to assist in tipping the process in your favor. The HR departments began screening applicants, using sophisticated software to look for keywords in the resume before proceeding to the next step. This made the process more sterile and took the relationship out of the decision process. Applicants started placing keywords in their resumes, first in the body of the resumes and then later as undetectable words on the resume that the scanner would pick up (using white font in the headers or footers for the scanner to read). The recruiters evolved and began adding assessment tests to the front of the process as a screening process. If the applicant didn't score well enough on the assessment, he/she didn't move on.

Jack was definitely not prepared for the assessment tests. He'd always done well on the standardized testing but this was different somehow. And, that was a long time ago and these modern job assessment tests had several parts. Some tests were timed, adding another level of stress to the process.

Jack still didn't have a confidant except Kathy, and even though he understood that he was not in control, he still felt the pressure and stress of finding a job. If he had someone else he could confide in, someone who understood his situation and what he was feeling, he wouldn't get depressed as easily.

The months rolled on and what was to be a couple of weeks, now seemed like it would take forever. Jack was losing faith. He was starting to think that he wouldn't find another job at all. Before, he thought he would find a job, but it would just take time. He prayed for guidance and he considered all possible solutions like starting his own business (although he wasn't an entrepreneur), finding several jobs to make ends meet (although working at an hourly job will take away from his job search); he was back to thinking about an entry-level job (although he hadn't realized that companies won't hire him because he was over-qualified and they feared he would leave if a new opportunity came along.) The anxiety had never really left. It was just below the surface, waiting for a weak moment to resurface.

"How did it go today?" Kathy asked.

"Pretty good. I researched a couple of new companies that are in a growth mode. I couldn't find anyone there that I know personally but I reached out to a few people who might be able to make some introductions." Jack replied.

"What else?"

"That was about it for the day. I had a couple of follow-up calls but got voicemail. Nothing new on the job boards but I feel pretty good on the new companies I've found; it will just take time."

"We don't have time, Jack. It doesn't seem like you are making any progress. No new applications this week. No face-to-face interviews. Maybe we need to discuss some other options like relocation."

His shoulders slumped and he lowered his head. Kathy's response to his daily activity took him from the "pretty good" day back to feeling like a failure. Her expectations were much higher than Jack's. Reality had set in and he knew this process was slow. He was starting to lose it again.

Maybe he *wasn't* making enough progress. Jack thought maybe they should take radical steps: sell the second car; cancel the cable TV and Internet; refinance the house or maybe sell the house and move in with relatives until he has a new job; tap into his 401(k). Maybe they *had* been living beyond their means, and now he wanted the course to correct overnight. This would make him feel like he was taking the necessary steps to conserve funds before they were out of money. Jack thought he was being rational, but he had slipped back into the panic mode. His trust in God didn't last.

The first sign of a challenge to his efforts and he was back to thinking *he* was in control, only trusting himself. Some of his ideas *were* coming from God. He really needed someone who had been through this to listen to and to challenge his thought process, but who? Jack had briefly met with a counselor, but she had not been where Jack was now, and she'd rarely counseled people in transition or read about the process and the effects. He needed someone who had lived this situation.

new opportunities

Jack had good days and bad days. He found that once he "let go" and just practiced the "right" behaviors without feeling desperate, things changed.   He began to receive feedback from potential employers in the form of meetings and interviews. He took the approach that not every interview was going to be a good fit but with an open mind, he could learn something in every interview.

He applied for a position in industrial sales, even though he had no background in this area. If he could land an interview, he would get some real practice at interviewing and that wasn't a bad thing. It also got him out of the house. His resume and telephone interview were enough to get him to the next round. He was invited in for an interview. He started his preparation and learned as much as he could about the company and the role for which he was interviewing. He was nervous because he had never sold this type of product/service, but he went anyway. The Human Resource person told him he would be interviewing with five people. Jack tried to find out as much about them as possible: LinkedIn connections, company website, Facebook, anything that could help him in making a connection.

Jack arrived at the company and was escorted to the HR Department. He met the HR Director and noticed another person in the office as well. Jack was a little confused and his face must've conveyed that confusion. The HR Director informed Jack that she was waiting on one other applicant and then she would escort all of them to the conference room. *What?* Jack was caught off guard. He asked how many people would be interviewing and she told him there were five people interviewing and five interviewers. This would be a group interview to be conducted simultaneously. *What?* Not only was Jack unprepared for this scenario, he had never heard of a group interview process before. It was the most bizarre practice he had ever heard of: five people, all being interviewed at the same time by a panel of five people. Crazy. He was ready to bolt for the door. While they were waiting for one more person, he decided he didn't have anything else on today, so he might as well stick it out.

They proceeded to the conference room and, sure enough, two other candidates were seated on one side of the table and three people on the other side of the table. To make this even more bizarre, two of the Interviewers were joining via Skype. They explained the process that each question would be asked with potential follow-up questions. The candidate to go first would be rotated so that each candidate would have a turn at going first.

He was ready to bolt again until they introduced the candidates and one of the names sounded familiar to Jack. He hadn't met the person, but he recognized the name. He decided to stay and catch up after the interview process.

Jack was asked the first question and as luck would have it, he had some experience with the subject. Jack used his expertise in this area and the other candidates, while they had experience in the industrial sales, had no experience in this subject. It was unlikely he would get this job, but he was getting valuable practice he couldn't get anywhere else.

The interview ended, and Jack connected with the candidate he was staying to meet. They spent time discussing the process and where each of them was in their job search. The other candidate was extremely well-qualified for the position. The expectation was that the company would notify those candidates who would be progressing to the next round in a few days. The few days turned into less than a day, and Jack had made it to the next round. He wasn't sure why since some of the others were more qualified. More practice at interviewing. He could use it.

When Jack showed up for the interview, his new friend's car was already in the parking lot. He made it to this round as well. Jack arrived at the HR Director's office and learned that the choice was between him and his friend.

Jack met with the President. Jack realized that he wasn't a good fit for this position and rather than continue to pursue this opportunity, he confided in the President that his friend would be the "right" choice. Jack decided to run interference for his new friend to eliminate the other competition. His friend got the job, and Jack felt great about helping someone get a job where they would do well.

The experience gave Jack a new appreciation for the "fit" of the organization with the individual. He didn't let his desperation force him to take a job that wasn't a good fit. He still gave it his best effort, but he knew he was not the right person. These events now gave him the ability to really focus on those opportunities that were a "fit" and that attitude served him well as he started to get more interviews with companies where he could excel. With this new confidence and more practice on the assessment testing, Jack started to get more meetings and more opportunities. He had his "best few" of opportunities where he was in the running, where he could not only add value, but the job would be a good fit, and he would be happy with the position and the company.

There were several opportunities from a variety of sources. They weren't offers but he made it through the initial round. Two opportunities came through job boards which shouldn't happen because all of the research said that no one was hired from a job posting. But Jack had two legitimate opportunities. A recruiter contacted him with another opportunity and a friend had reached out with a contact that was looking for someone with Jack's skills and experience. Jack started to stack rank the companies without even having an initial interview. He was deselecting himself from an opportunity that hadn't been offered.

"I've been thinking about this new opportunity, and I don't think I'm a good fit. I think I should take myself out of the running," Jack said to Kathy.

"Why would you eliminate yourself and not even try?" Kathy asked him bluntly. "How can you be so sure you're not a good fit even before the interview?"

"Maybe you're right. Maybe I should let it play out and see where it goes. If the fit is good for me and the company, God will take care of the direction," Jack replied.

Kathy's advice was good advice, and Jack refocused his efforts to approach each opportunity as if it were the best opportunity he would be presented.

He was ready to go, and, of the four opportunities, two required an online assessment test prior to getting the first face-to-face interview. Jack wasn't concerned until he saw the test. These were the tests that

Jack had heard about. The ones like the ACT. These tests were timed with sections on math, logic, English, and psychology. So much for hiding the keywords in the resume to get past the screener. Jack knew these tests were legit and would deselect candidates who didn't post an acceptable score. He was nervous. His personality, experience, and skills would not come through on an objective test like this.

Jack had not taken any standardized test in a long time, and there was really no way to prepare. He tapped his pencil and fidgeted in his seat. Jack wondered if the test would be simple, asking simple math questions or obvious psychological questions; or would this be a nightmare with complex math and psychological questions that could be answered a number of ways. There was no easy way to ensure he moved to the next round.

Jack began the first online assessment test and he had one hour to complete the four sections. Each section was timed and at the end of the section one, the screen would time out and take him to the next section. The instructions included a statement that made it very plain: "You will NOT complete any of the individual sections within the allotted time." Not the result that Jack anticipated. Jack wouldn't know if he completed 80% of the test or 50% of the test. This was more stressful than he thought.

Jack moved on to the next round in the process. He finished the testing phase on the two opportunities, and he was anticipating face-to-face interviews. He hadn't interviewed in a very long time, but he remembered the preparation. Jack had his "third-party stories" ready to provide examples of his experience in specific situations. He found an Internet site regarding how to prepare for an interview and he had those written down. He had to remember that his objective was to get to the next round. Telephone interviews would weed out candidates that didn't need to be interviewed face-to-face.

Jack was usually pretty good on the telephone and his personality came through. Over the next couple of weeks, Jack had four telephone interviews and had moved on to the next round with face-to-face interviews. He had stopped prospecting for any new opportunities. One of these four would be a fit. He was confident that he could do all four of the positions based on his prior experience and, at this point, he was selling himself on why each of them would be a good fit. He believed that God was in control and he just needed to have a positive attitude and do his best. One of these opportunities *would* work out.

Jack arrived at his first interview with GP Technology, a global positioning technology company that was looking for a manager to run their insides sales group, and he was meeting with the Human Resource Manager who was responsible for all new talent. He was not meeting with the hiring manager at this point, which would come only after another screening process. The HR person was young enough to be one of his kids, and she had her standard set of questions for all candidates. Unfortunately, some of the questions didn't make sense for someone like Jack.

"Where do you want to be in ten years?" she asked.

I want to be retired in ten years, he thought, but he couldn't say that. Jack responded, "I'd like to be making a significant contribution to my company, helping to grow the company and the people I work with." It probably sounded fake, but he couldn't say what he was really thinking.

The interview proceeded with more standard questions and Jack gave the answers he thought would satisfy the HR rep. Eventually, she invited Jack to ask questions. The questions Jack had written down from his preparation were designed more for the hiring manager than a screener from HR. But Jack asked anyway and most of the responses were, "That's a great question. I don't have the specifics on that. That would be something you could ask the hiring manager." Jack had to remind himself that his objective was to get to the next round. He left the interview feeling just okay. Not great. He didn't know who he was meeting with, what the process was going to be, and had questions that weren't pertinent for the person who was interviewing him. He had to do a better job the next time.

Jack moved on to the next face-to-face interview with Network Payment Solutions (NPS), a payment platform company that came from one of the job boards. He'd done research and had better clarification from the telephone interview to know that he would be interviewing with the hiring manager. He realized that the hiring manager worked with a friend of his in a prior position. He reached out to his friend to find out about this hiring manager.

Jack set up a meeting to catch up and learn what he could about the person who would be interviewing him. He learned about his personal life; his work ethic; what he looked for in his team; how long he had been with the company; how he got to this position. He asked his friend for a recommendation, and if he could reach out and put in a good word for him.

He had his interview with NPS and met with the Senior Vice President of Sales and Marketing, Jim. The position was for a Vice

President of Sales and this would be a good fit for Jack based on his experience in managing sales groups and he knew a little something about payment networks. He felt more prepared for this interview and the interview was more conversational which put Jack at ease. He worked into the conversation that his friend Bill was a friend of Jim's. Jim said he received a call from Bill, and they discussed how each of them knows Bill. Jack left the interview feeling pretty good. This interview was an improvement over the last one but didn't go as well as it could have gone. Maybe Jack was trying to convince himself that no matter what the job was, he could make it work. He may not have the passion for it, but it would do. He would settle for the position. This position was considerably less than where he was in salary and he found out that it was also a sales producer position in addition to managing sales people. Jim recommended to Jack that they should meet again in a couple of weeks after the company had moved into its new offices.

Better, but still not great. *What am I doing wrong?* He really wanted to feel that as he left the interview, he could picture himself in that position. So far, he hadn't had that feeling.

Jack had two more interviews and he felt good about them. A couple of days passed, and he didn't hear anything on any of the positions. He looked on the job boards and all four positions were still posted, so he assumed they were still accepting candidates. He reached out to GP Technology to see where they were in the process. The HR Manager from GP Technology informed Jack that he would not be moving to the next step. They felt he was overqualified for the position. *What?* Wouldn't taking a significant step down in both salary and position make it easier for a company to hire him? Instead, it had the opposite effect. He was *too* qualified for the position.

Jack had wasted a couple of weeks of prospecting an opportunity that would not hire him because he was over qualified. He had lost ground and needed to update his job-prospecting efforts to determine how a company views someone with considerable experience. He also needed to determine what went wrong in the interview with GP Technology. Was it really that he was overqualified and, if it was, why was that an issue? Did they think he would continue to look for new positions at other companies that were a better fit for his experience? Was he more qualified than his boss and the boss would be threatened by that?

Jack continued to search for opportunities in several areas because he didn't want to "deselect" himself before he even had an offer. Plus, he wanted to get more real-life experience in the hiring process of assessments, telephone interviews, and face-to-face interviews.   He was still too "all over the place" in his prospecting because the process was taking far longer than he had anticipated. He was staying positive but the length of time it was taking was wearing on him. Even the time in the interview and hiring process was taking longer than he had expected. He thought that once a company had the first round of interviews and assessments, they would make a decision. So far, that had not been the process. There were multiple steps with weeks in between.

He had been trying to follow up with NPS because he thought that was a role he could step into and immediately make a contribution. He understood the market and the product; he had already thought through a prospecting plan for new business; his friend Bill had recommended him for the position so what was going on? It was radio silence from the company. He was chasing them for some kind of feedback and now he might sound desperate or like he was a pest. If he was not a good fit, he just wanted to know so he could move on. He was in limbo on this one.

Jack finally connected with a friend at GP Technology that had assisted in getting him the initial interview and they met for coffee. It was totally off the record, but his friend wanted him to know what was going on. The interview went great. They liked his knowledge and experience and they believed his personality would be a good fit with their culture. Now for the bad news. Number one, they were concerned about his age. Did Jack have the drive and energy to bring new business to GP Technology? They thought he might be looking for a position that was the last chapter before retirement, and they needed someone who would be around for several years to make a contribution. Funny. The company would rather hire a millennial that would be with them for two years max before moving on to their next job versus someone who would stay with them to grow the company. The company's perceptions were not reality, but they weren't going to be convinced.

Number two, the company was concerned that Jack was so overqualified that not only was his would-be boss intimidated, but the company was worried that Jack would continue to look for another position that better suited his prior experience and level of authority. This wasn't what Jack wanted to hear but it *was* good feedback. He now understood that he was fighting an age issue on a couple of fronts

– length of time remaining with the company and the energy/vitality he had to commit to the company. He suspected that Human Resources may have had an issue as well with hiring an older employee in terms of healthcare costs. Jack had never had to deal with this before. It wasn't about his ability or experience, it was about battling perceptions. His interviewing skills would have to change.

Not surprisingly, his anxiety returned. Jack's age, experience and level of achievement were now working against him. He listened to himself again and thought the worse – he would not get another job. As soon as he made it to the interview stage, he'd lose. Jack still had two other opportunities in play, but he realized he must understand where his REAL strengths were and pursue positions where he could make a contribution. He had to get to a decision maker that understood the value Jack could bring and then they would begin to see the benefits. His interviewing style must change. He had been relying on "feature and benefits" much like the old sales process. He had to reinvent himself to better communicate the value that he would bring. The new process would focus on the company and not on Jack's skills and experience. He needed to develop the new process and stick with it.

First, his prospecting had to change. He had been selling himself on what he had done and the success he has had. He was out of work. If the company had seen that value, why did they let him go? His approach was going to change to focus on what he did and who he had typically worked with along with a question regarding the relevance to the company.

Jack worked on a couple of different introductions. "Hi, my name is Jack Thompson, and I was referred to you by Jim Marshall. I'm sure I'm catching you at a bad time. "

"I don't know if it makes sense, but I thought that maybe we could spend a few minutes face-to-face learning more about each other. For our meeting, I'd like to ask some questions and I'm sure you'll have some as well. At the end of the meeting, we can go one of two directions, either we determine that we are a good fit and we can continue discussions or, we'll determine it's not a good fit and we can part ways. Will that work for you?"

"I typically work with companies that are frustrated by their current sales results, have plateaued in their topline revenues, need to enter new vertical markets without significantly increasing cost, and increase their valuation. Is any of that relevant for you?"

Now that he had a new approach that could be used for prospecting calls and emails, he had to find someone who needed the value he could bring, not try to convince someone that he could add value. His approach was to "go for the no." It sounded counterintuitive, but he couldn't waste his time going through the interview process only to find out that the company was looking for someone younger and cheaper.

This new approach was difficult for Jack. His experience in the hiring process had always been to qualify the candidate and let them interview with multiple people to see if the collective decision was to hire them. This approach reversed the roles and the interviewee was really taking control and trying to determine if this was a good fit. He was skeptical this would work. It was way too "out there." The experts suggested you restructured your resume so that it focused on value but that too seemed hard to do. He had to try something because he was not getting the results he needed.

The whole process was taking too long, and it had been four and a half months of job searching. What Jack thought would take a couple of weeks had stretched into almost twenty. He felt like he was out of contacts and networking was getting tougher. Kathy was losing patience and still couldn't understand what he did all day. The kids were really in the dark because Jack hadn't shared anything with them. Their friends were all working and doing really well. You would think that someone with Jack's skill set would not have a problem finding a new position.

Jack began using the new approach and although he was uncomfortable, he was having some success. The approach was less threatening because he set the rules up front that if this was not a good fit, they would both move on. The people he talked to appreciated his honesty, and he didn't seem desperate to get a job. Jack received a new opportunity – way outside his previous industry and his experience but the company was looking for someone who could accelerate what they already had in place. Jack went to work on making connections with people at the company and at the firm doing the search. Could *this* be it? It sounded like a fit, but he hadn't met anyone at the company yet. The search firm was handling the screening process.

Jack learned not to put all of his efforts into one opportunity, but he had developed a plan for the next stage of the process. This process was more extensive than what he had seen in the past, requiring patience and perseverance to stay focused on this opportunity and still pursue others as well. He made it through the initial telephone interview and created rapport with the interviewer. He also made it through the initial assessment test. His next step was a face-to-face interview with the search firm and the person he was interviewing with was a friend of a friend. He reached out to his friend to see how well he knew the person who would be interviewing him to see if he could use him as a reference. The mutual friend could at least be a starting point in building rapport with another person at the search firm. He began the research on the search firm and the hiring company to learn as much as he could and maybe even talk to some people who were familiar with one of the companies. He needed leverage which would come from learning what he could, followed by asking good questions about what he didn't know.

Jack had multiple opportunities in various stages—from telephone interviews to assessment testing to face-to-face. He needed to keep his pipeline full. He also didn't want to "fall in love" with one opportunity. Putting too much focus on one opportunity limited his prospecting and networking efforts and he had to start over if that opportunity wasn't a fit.

It had now been six months since his job was eliminated, and Jack felt like it was only yesterday that he sat in the parking lot with that Bankers Box on the seat next to him. He was still having sleepless nights, but he was finding more ways to be frugal. He considered getting rid of cable TV since it was a luxury they could do without. He had already consolidated cell phone plans for a lower monthly expense. He wasn't playing golf, and he and Kathy were not going on vacations. He canceled a trip with his friends that he had attended for the last twenty years – he just couldn't justify it. He thought of selling the house and buying something smaller while the interest rates were still low. He could also change to a 30-year fixed rate versus the 15-year fixed rate he had currently and reduce his monthly payment. If he could reduce his expenses, they could live on less income and accept a position that was a couple of levels below where he was. Nothing was off the table. All expenses were being considered. He needed to move forward with several to conserve cash. No telling how long this would last. The unemployment benefits he was receiving would eventually run out and he didn't want to be surprised when they did. He had already dipped way too far into his savings to maintain the lifestyle he and Kathy had been living.

Done and done. The house was on the market. The plan was to sell the current house, put the furniture in storage and move in with a relative while they searched for another house. That way, there was no pressure to coordinate a move and they could be selective in buying a house. The challenge was that he had to be working to qualify for a loan. He might be living with relatives longer than he expected.

One of his opportunities was still progressing and he was getting down to the finals. The position was between Jack and one other applicant. He felt like this would be a good fit for him to utilize his skills and experience. They weren't worried about his age but were looking for leadership. Perfect. The final steps were a face-to-face presentation on case studies and then one final assessment and interview with an outside firm. Another month and a half to two months because of travel schedules. It was all testing his patience.

Jack was prepared on the case studies. He had done his homework and he had thought through his 90-day plan to get up to speed.

The last step was an assessment followed by a face-to-face with a psychologist. The assessment was supposed to last about four to four-and-a-half hours. *What could possibly take that long?* He was all scheduled for the test and many of the sections were timed with instructions that "you will not finish." They were right. This assessment was the hardest he had taken. It was harder than the standard college acceptance test. The test lasted four and a half hours, and Jack was exhausted afterward. Two sections on math, both timed; an English section; a logic section; a personality section, and a psychological section. The final phase was in four days. Jack still had other opportunities but none that were this far along in the process.

The final step (he hoped) was the interview with the psychologist. Jack had decided that rather than attempt to anticipate the questions and have the "perfect" answer, he was going to be transparent and answer the questions truthfully without vagueness or ambiguity.

The interviewer, Dr. Bluestein, was tough. No building rapport here. He sat straight in his chair and was all business. He didn't even look down at his computer while he typed responses to questions. An hour into the interview, they were still going. An interview question came up regarding stress.

"Jack, how do you handle stress? What do you do to relieve the stress that is part of all of our lives?" asked Dr. Bluestein.

Jack couldn't say that he ran half marathons or that he didn't have stress. He had to tell the truth, or it would come off as insincere.

"I sit in church," Jack said.

"What?" asked Dr. Bluestein.

"I sit in church. It is the most peaceful place on earth, and I can sit for 30 minutes or an hour and all of the stress goes away."

"Okay," said Dr. Bluestein. "That's the end of the interview. Do you have any questions for me?"

"When will the decision be made and are there any more steps in the process?"

"This is the last step in the process, but I don't know when a final decision will be made."

Jack called Kathy on the way home, and she asked how it went.

"Well, I thought it was going pretty well until the interviewer asked how I handle stress."

"Why? What did you say?" Kathy asked.

"I told him I sit in church. I could have said an Adoration Chapel, but I kept it at just 'church.'"

"How did he react?"

"He didn't have much of a reaction. He asked me to repeat my answer like he didn't hear me the first time, so maybe I confused him."

"At least you were truthful, and if you don't get this job because of that, it was meant to be—there is something else out there for you."

Always the optimist. Kathy had been his rock during this phase of his life and had not complained and was constantly supportive.

Jack didn't stop his prospecting, but he felt pretty good about this opportunity. Two days later, he received an offer letter. Jack was relieved and ecstatic. He could finally go back to work and use his talents and experience to accelerate the processes that were already in place. The long dry spell was over. He had a couple of weeks before he would be starting the job, but he could put this prospecting behind him.

anxiety iv

His first day of work was filled with meeting people and completing paperwork. Jack was anxious to get started so he arrived early. Getting back to work after months of prospecting for a new position, Jack was ready to go. He hadn't been in this industry before, so he didn't have the knowledge base that he had after years and years with his last company.

The first week was a whirlwind. He attended several internal meetings to discuss current and prospective clients. The discussion centered on the contact people and the relationship. The discussion included competition and what they were doing. Jack was lost. Really lost. He wasn't familiar with the client base, competitors, pricing models, length of contract, not even the services provided He thought this would be easier. Week one turned into week two and then month one. He was still not up to speed. Jack was afraid to ask obvious questions, but he really didn't know what was being discussed. He should be picking this up more quickly.

Jack felt like he wouldn't catch up quick enough. *What if this was a bad move?* He thought this was a good fit, but he underestimated the complexity of the business and how long it might take to learn all of the clients and contacts names and organizational charts. He felt inadequate. He wondered if his boss was second-guessing himself on hiring him. He knew that he wasn't hired because of his industry knowledge, but he couldn't help feeling like he was the dumbest person in the room. How long would they give him before they expected he would be up to speed?

Again, he wasn't sleeping at night. He feared that another job elimination was around the corner. He'd only been with the new company for a couple of months, but he didn't feel like he was making the immediate contribution he thought he would make. He tried to be pragmatic. Before the loss of his job, Jack had never been through a job elimination, and now he feared it would happen again. Was this something that happened more frequently at a certain age or was it the economy? What was driving these negative feelings? Jack realized he must get out of this mindset or it would become a self-fulfilling prophecy. He had to be more realistic.

The more Jack attended meetings with others in the company, the more inadequate he felt. He couldn't keep all of the clients and contacts straight. He had never felt like this before. When would he catch on? Six months? A year? How long would his new boss tolerate it? He should be asking about his performance to date, but he was afraid of the answer. His emotional health was not where it should be. He was still on that roller coaster and couldn't seem to get off. He expected that with the new job, the highs and lows would quit, that he could get off the roller coaster and he would be happy, but he was still battling the anxiety.

emotional health

Jack needed to stop the swings from joy to anxiety, but he didn't know how. He needed peace. He couldn't do this on his own and he needed to find some balance.

He remembered where he was just a short time ago: his work came first. His career, his job, earning a living and providing Kathy and the kids with everything they wanted. But he was first in his priority list. Always had been. Of course, when someone asked, he gave the answer that most people expected: "I put my wife and kids first." He knew that was a lie.

Jack went from the anxiety of not having a job to the temporary pleasure of landing a job, and back to the anxiety of feeling this job may not have been a good fit and that he'd made a mistake by accepting the position. Jack recalled the retreat that seemed so long ago. He thought he was in control and learned that he wasn't. He had to let go and trust in God, and he had to recover this trust again.

This was a process that he had been working on since the retreat, growing to be less self-centered. He even stayed on to participate in the next retreat, working with men in similar stages of life. But now, when he thought everything would be fine after landing a new job, he was aware of how shallow his faith really was, and how he still didn't trust that God would take care of him.

It took a job elimination to get his attention the first time. He couldn't let the fear of losing a job shake his faith that easily. He decided to pick up where he left off. After the retreat, he changed some bad habits but as time went on, he found himself falling into the same old routine.

He needed a refresher on how to let go and trust. First, he started going to Mass more frequently again, maybe once or twice a week and not just on Sunday. He also needed to prepare for Mass: read the readings, read some reflections, try to understand what God was trying to say to him. Jack compared it to a business meeting where his boss told him the time and place and provided the background information to prepare. He wouldn't think of walking into that meeting not having read the information and researched the topic so he could participate in the meeting. But he'd never done that for Mass. He typically showed up and waited to be inspired. If he wasn't inspired, it was the priest's fault. The homily was bad, the priest was not a good communicator, the music was too low, whatever the excuse. He needed to get back into the habit of Mass and preparation.

Jack eventually became more comfortable in his new job and his emotional health improved. He found more balance in his life, a life that had previously been out of balance. He was now more aware. Rather than walking around anticipating another job elimination, he started living his life. Thriving, not just surviving.

He resolved to do the best he could in his current job, ask questions, and stop worrying about losing his job or disappointing his boss and focus on his development as a person: husband, father, brother, neighbor, friend, coworker, employee, mentor, and coach.

Then – and only then – could his life become the full and happy one to which he aspired.

THE SUPPORT

spouse, caregiver & significant other

When a job elimination occurs, the first thing we all need to do is to share this with our spouse. We'll refer to them as "spouse," but it could be a significant other or even a caregiver. It's someone who shares our life, someone that we trust without reservation. Some of us tend to keep our emotions bottled up, not displaying our perceived weakness. The result is increased anxiety, sleep loss, and mild to severe depression. Sometimes we are embarrassed by the job elimination, blaming ourselves as if we have some character flaw or we deserved to be let go because of our performance. This is never true, or we'd be more open and matter-of-fact about it. We're not. We're in shock. We want to hold this all inside when the first thing we should do is to share our feelings.

Not sharing what happens in a job elimination and the feelings associated with the process effectively shuts out the one person that we can rely on to be non-judgmental of us. On some occasions, our spouse will not understand and think that we did something wrong, but most often they will skip the shock step and go straight to anger. They may never leave that stage. Our spouse sees the after-effects of the job elimination: the sleepless nights, the lack of self-esteem, the uncertainty of the future earnings. They want someone to pay, an emotional payment, to hurt like the eliminated person is hurting. They want retribution.

Sharing our emotions and feelings lets our spouse know what is going on with us. We may have shared the mechanics of the job elimination and the job search, but we need to let down our guard and share our true feelings. When we do, we bring our spouse into the process. We cannot lock them out of the emotional side. We also need to be cautious when we begin to share what we are feeling and not "dump" on our spouse, expecting them to take away our anxiety. They can be sympathetic but not empathetic unless they have felt the same pains associated with a job loss and the same sense of failure that the "head of household" would feel.

When we are open and share our experiences, our spouses can be supportive and celebrate the small victories like getting an interview or getting a networking meeting. They also can keep us grounded so we don't dwell too much on failure and the unsuccessful attempts at meetings or the interviews that don't go as well as we would have liked.

When the job search goes longer than you expect and frustration creeps in, your spouse may not be as sympathetic as they once were. We have to remember that they never entered the anxiety phase and have been angry since the job elimination. If they work outside the home and come home after work, they may ask, "How was your day?" If you spent the day doing research on companies and people, making phone calls and sending emails, you may not have made much real progress. Your spouse may equate productivity with activity and if they don't see a full schedule of interviews and meetings, they might wonder, "What did you do all day?"

It's important to set some realistic expectations. The rule-of-thumb a few years ago was that for every $10,000 in salary, it takes one month to find a position. That means, if you were making $100,000 a year, you could expect your job search to take at least ten months. This can obviously be influenced by the industry, geographic location, and title but it is a starting point to set expectations. Don't beat yourself up too much but don't just assume the new job will mysteriously find you. It is hard work. There is a lot of competition for jobs and as unemployment drops, you may have several opportunities. When unemployment increases, you are less marketable.

If you aren't having an ongoing dialogue with your significant other, you're shutting them out. They already know that you're not sleeping at night. When you're depressed, they know. When you start to consider selling the house and "buying down" or canceling the cable television, newspaper, Netflix, or other subscriptions, they know. Share. Make your spouse part of the conversation. They might be the voice of reason.

Sometimes, you will have to make a change in your finances (canceling a service or cutting back an expense) just to feel like you are doing everything you can to be more frugal and conserve cash. Share that feeling with your spouse. They need to understand that it may seem insignificant, but you need to do it for your own sanity.

mentor

Another person you'll need to find when a job elimination occurs is a mentor. Your mentor is someone who can provide you with direction and a plan. Your mentor is someone who can assist with behaviors (networking, meetings, interviewing) and techniques (resume, social media, LinkedIn, job boards). This person is important because they have knowledge that you may not have. They have a different perspective. They may be in the same industry or a different one. They may be at the same organizational level or above your last position. They may be more connected than you and may see the world differently.

Your mentor will not only provide needed direction but could also challenge you when you start to rationalize irrational ideas, and you will. As the job search goes on, you will be tempted to start thinking about alternatives that months before would have sounded like crazy ideas. Some of those might be okay and will work. Others are just that, crazy ideas, and your mentor can help you decide which are which. Two of those ideas that will cross your mind are whether to become your own boss or whether you should take a position that would be one or several steps below your last position. These ideas creep in almost every time.

First, you think, I don't need to be the _____ (VP of whatever, Director, Senior Assistant Vice President). You have convinced yourself to start looking at open positions that you may have done earlier in your career and could do today without much training. You'd be an immediate benefit to the company. You would be an asset to your boss, having done his/her job in the past. Guess what? The likelihood of getting that job is very slim. You will be overqualified, and the hiring manager will presume that you consider the job a stop-gap until you find one that better suits your experience and skills. It won't matter that you have mentally prepared yourself to take the step down.

You want less stress. You want to go back to work. You want to be productive. You want to feel needed. Doesn't matter. In the long run, the hiring manager or the human resource manager or someone else will still have in the back of their mind that you'll continue to look for another job.

This may not be the case. You may feel morally obligated to stay with the company that helped you out when you needed the job. You may have already run and rerun and run again all of your finances and you know what you can live on and where you will have to make lifestyle changes. Still doesn't matter. If you believe the research on hiring, take the position salary and multiply it by a factor of six to get the real cost of a bad hire. If you thought, "I can take that job that only pays $60,000 even though I was making $100,000 before," the company is thinking, "If we hire this guy and he doesn't work out for whatever reason, we cost ourselves $360,000; we should have moved on and looked for the right person." Companies, even smaller companies today, are using caution when making hiring decisions. That may change in the upcoming years as the labor pool gets smaller, but companies are going to be more selective because they understand the true cost of hiring. Most companies today use at least one assessment test in their hiring practice and this could come well before a telephone interview occurs. If you don't meet the criteria for Must

Haves, Should Haves, and Nice to Haves, you won't ever see the interview stage.

The other thought process that might occur to you is to "be your own boss." This comes in several forms from purchasing a franchise to expanding a hobby. Be careful. Being your own boss is not as easy as it sounds and it's not for everyone. Being an entrepreneur is hard work. Lots of hours for little or no pay while you're ramping up your business. If the cost of entry is low, the return on your sweat equity could be as well. Look at the restaurant business. How many people do you know who want to or have opened a restaurant? It sounds easy. You have a great concept, a great location, you've run the numbers and it all looks good. In your research, don't forget to look at the failure rate of restaurants. Not that some don't make it – they do – but those are the ones where someone had realistic expectations, started slow, learned, adjusted, and wasn't desperate. It's like that with any business. Franchises take some of that planning out for you because they've already tested the concept and they have support, but you pay for that support as well. Owning your own business entails many hours and the work becomes your life, so if you want to spend time at the lake, or play golf, travel, coach your kids, watch your grandkids play sports, anything like that, you'll have to shelve that until your business is profitable.

Your mentor is important because they should be able to challenge, not just agree, with you. They should not be your "Yes Man," but rather a sounding board that takes the emotion out of decisions you might make and then walks you through the process to test it. You may find that you've always been an entrepreneur and you can take the side business you have been doing for the last ten years and expand it into a full-time business. Your mentor may have an idea how you can mentor a new company (actually taking a position below where you have been accustomed) to accelerate the company and support the person in charge. Your mentor can help you find a way to communicate and construct a position that provides you with less stress and the company with experience and skills so that both parties win, and the company isn't waiting for you to find another job.

Find that mentor. He/she doesn't have to be a friend but if they are, they have to be open and honest with you. No watching out for your feelings; you have your spouse for that.

counselor

Your counselor is the person you can confide in regarding the entire process of the job elimination and the job search. Unlike your spouse, your counselor is someone who has walked in these shoes. Ideally, your counselor is someone who has been through a job elimination. They know firsthand what it feels like. They know the loneliness of looking for a new job, the lack of interaction with other people. They know how uncomfortable you feel when someone asks, "How's the job search going?" They know the feeling when you are interviewing, and the other candidates are half your age and will take half the salary you were making. They know how the interview process has changed and how you need to prepare.

Sometimes, you'll find a counselor who can also be a mentor to you. Bonus! Don't underestimate the value of a counselor. This is your coach. The counselor is going to work on part of your attitude. They may not focus on behaviors and techniques; they want your head in the game. Attitude is 80% of your success. You can have the best behaviors and techniques and still not find that position that will be the next chapter in your career. Conversely, if your attitude is positive and you are focused on the fit (not desperate for any job), it can overcome less-than-perfect behaviors and techniques. Attitude is everything.

spiritual director

Not everyone is going to agree about this role, but it is as important as the other roles, maybe more so. If you don't have faith in something, the job elimination and the new job search will be infinitely more difficult. Without faith, you are left to your own devices so ALL your successes and ALL of your failures are yours and yours alone. When you don't get to the interview stage, it's on you. When you get to the interview and no further, it's on you. When you have a spiritual director, he/she can keep you grounded to understand that you are not in control. Sure, you get to make all kinds of decisions, but you can't control the outcomes of those decisions. You may have a pretty good idea of what might happen, and you might TRY to control it, but in the end, you don't control it.

Have you ever made a decision and you were sure it was the right way to go and you knew exactly how things would turn out but then they didn't turn out that way? It's because you are not in control. You never have been, and you never will be.

Now, that doesn't mean that you can sit around, and good things will just happen for you. You need to put in the hard work to allow things to happen. You can't sit on the couch and expect the phone to ring with a great offer for your next opportunity.

Here's a story by an unknown author that illustrates the point.

I SENT YOU A ROWBOAT

A very religious man was once caught in rising floodwaters. He climbed onto the roof of his house and trusted God to rescue him. A neighbor came by in a canoe and said, "The waters will soon be above your house. Hop in and we'll paddle to safety."

"No, thanks," replied the religious man. "I've prayed to God and I'm sure he will save me."

A short time later the police came by in a boat. "The waters will soon be above your house. Hop in and we'll take you to safety."

"No, thanks," replied the religious man. "I've prayed to God and I'm sure he will save me."

A little time later a rescue services helicopter hovered overhead, let down a rope ladder and said,. "The waters will soon be above your house. Climb the ladder and we'll fly you to safety."

"No, thanks," replied the religious man. "I've prayed to God and I'm sure he will save me."

All this time the floodwaters continued to rise, until soon they reached above the roof and the religious man drowned. When he arrived in heaven, he demanded an audience with God. Ushered into God's throne room, he said, "Lord, why am I here in heaven? I prayed for you to save me, I trusted you to save me from that flood."

"Yes, you did, my child," replied the Lord. "And I sent you a canoe, a boat and a helicopter. But you never got in."

Without a spiritual director, you might be sitting on a two-legged stool. You can balance there for a while but eventually, it gets harder and harder to maintain your balance. Some people may think they have a spiritual director and their faith is strong, but they are just going through the motions. Now, they have a three-legged stool but one of the legs is much shorter than the others, and again it's hard to keep your balance. For this to be effective, you must have faith, and your spiritual director should be someone who can remind you that this is not ALL on your shoulders. There are no coincidences and when you don't get the interview, another opportunity is waiting. When you don't get the job offer, another one will come that is a better fit.

The people who find this transition easier to cope with are those who have faith in God. God always answers our prayers, just not with the answers we always anticipate. Maybe when you were busy focused on your career and title and status and compensation, your spouse was praying for you to be a better person and not so much of a jackass. What they thought was that you would have some epiphany and become a better person and maybe what really happened was that your job was eliminated, and you had time to reflect on what a jackass you have been. God answered your spouse's prayer, just not the way anyone expected. You may think this is crazy, but I know for a fact it happens.

Your spiritual director doesn't have to be a priest, pastor, reverend, or anyone else from the clergy. Your spiritual director must be someone who will be open and honest with you and truly believes in faith and prayer. The reason is because it works. When you are experiencing the stages of job elimination, you need someone who can speak the truth to you so that you don't put all of the pressure on yourself.

Do you know how liberating it is to walk into a job interview and realized that if this isn't the right fit, you'll know it; and, conversely, if it IS the right fit, you'll know that too? When you have an opportunity, you'll sometimes talk yourself into why this is a perfect fit. It may not be, but the desperation you feel may make you want to believe it. When it really *is* right, you will feel more energized, the words will flow more easily, and you will have clarity about how you will fit into this role.

MOVING ON

lessons learned

When a job elimination first occurs, the emotional impact is significant. Unfortunately, no one really discusses it. Everyone feels like this is abnormal, that people don't go through job eliminations. We all hear about them, but those are "other" people, not us. What we all fail to realize is that this is very normal. The job elimination is normal, the emotional reaction is normal, and the "not wanting to discuss it" is normal.

Jack's story is all too common. You work your way up the ladder, trading valuable family and personal time to promote a career, only to have the career end abruptly when the market takes a downturn.

Let's look at some lessons learned that can help avoid that blindside and better prepare you for a change even if it never comes.

In a November 13, 2013 article in Forbes magazine, Donna Ballman identified *"11 Sneaky Ways Companies Get Rid of Older Workers."* Donna is a Florida employment lawyer and identifies what "might" constitute age discrimination, but it is extremely difficult to prove and trying to fight age discrimination could be a distraction from moving on to the next chapter in a career. Here are Donna's 11 Ways:

1. **Job Elimination.** Companies can routinely reorganize and just eliminate positions that are no longer part of the organizational structure. Proving that this is targeting older employees is very difficult.

2. **Layoff.** Companies are supposed to attach to a layoff notice a list of other employees included and excluded from the layoff along with their ages. Some will show selected departments or

specific job titles and, more often, they will include a few under 40 to make this look less like age discrimination.

3. **Suddenly stupid**. You've had great performance reviews and suddenly, you are getting reprimanded for things that everyone does or being nitpicked for things that were never important. They may be building a case to get rid of you for poor performance.

4. **Threatening your pension**. This is usually a hollow threat and they may claim that you can lose your right to be vested if you're fired "for cause," but you have appeal rights if they deny benefits so it's not that easy.

5. **Early retirement**. These plans could make you an offer that's too good to pass up so review it carefully. If you decline it, you could still be fired at will.

6. **Mandatory retirement age**. If the employer has one of these, they're probably breaking the law. There are some exceptions, however.

7. **Cutting job duties**. One way to force older employees out is to cut job duties, limiting authority and humiliation with lower level tasks.

8. **Isolation**. Cutting you out of meetings, excluding you from lunches and sticking you in an area away from the action is a way to get you to quit.

9. **Denying promotions or opportunities for advancement**. Employers can't deny you a promotion because they think you will retire soon. If they cut your job duties and isolate you, they can justify that you are not qualified.

10. **Cutting hours**. Starving you to death is a way to get you to quit.

11. **Harassment**. Cutting job duties, isolation, and denying opportunities are all forms of harassment, as is constantly asking when you will retire.

Many of these "sneaky ways" might be tried to "deselect" (another euphemism for being eliminated, but it sounds like the employee made the decision) an employee who has been with the company for many years.

Be Aware.

If you have typically been a part of meetings (e.g. executive, strategy, financial) and you are no longer part of the group, this should create some awareness. Sometimes we see this as freedom not to attend meetings that cut into our day or created more work for us in an already-busy schedule. This could be an isolation tactic and positioned in such a way that you feel like your boss is freeing up some time for you. Probably not the case, and you should be aware that there could be a second agenda: that of creating an environment that alienates you from the group.

Another tactic that happens too often is when your job duties are cut. Again, the positioning is that you have too much on your plate and by cutting responsibilities, you can focus on fewer initiatives and produce better results.

Awareness is not paranoia. Being aware of the situation and objectively reviewing the situation will better prepare you in case it does lead to an elimination. Not being honest with yourself leads to a confirmation bias whereby you will only select information that supports your position rather than reviewing a situation objectively. In sales, it's sometimes referred to as "happy ears." We don't want to think this could be negative; therefore, we miss the signs that point to an eventual job elimination.

Share your feelings.

When we think this is a sign of failure or weakness or having done something wrong, we bottle up our feelings and don't want to talk about what's happening when this is exactly what we should be doing. We don't need to have pity parties on a routine basis, but we definitely should not push down all those feelings. We need to release them. That's why the support people mentioned earlier are important. You need to find those people who can listen and assist. They are not there to coddle; they're there to support and offer guidance and feedback. Use them. Don't ever think that other people aren't experiencing the same thing. When we ignore those feelings, we end up with unhealthy side effects. We may develop insomnia, panic attacks, depression and other physical effects. The bad news is: all of these side effects have a negative impact on our ability to move on and find our next opportunity.

The Greatest Generation experienced job eliminations just like the Baby Boomers have been experiencing them. The difference is that they repressed those feelings even more so than the Baby Boomers. Some of them self-medicated. They had grown up during the Great Depression, lived through WW II and Korea. Most couldn't afford much education and worked blue collar jobs. If they belonged to a union, they may have had some protection from a job elimination. For those who weren't protected, they may have chosen to turn to alcohol instead of discussing being out of work. They never thought to discuss their problems with someone else – they just pushed those feelings down and moved on. Not a healthy way to handle it but that's all they knew.

For the Baby Boomers, the American Dream was instilled in them by their parents and some of the truisms that we ascribed to are no longer true. The Greatest Generation associated a good job with being with the same company throughout their working careers. Part of that American Dream was to retire from your job and receive the gold watch as a token of your service and dedication to the company. Those days are gone. In the 1940's employees could expect to stay with the same company for 30 or 40 years, gold prices were at about $34 an ounce. Today, the average length of job tenure is five (5) years and gold prices are more like $1,300 an ounce (*Saying Goodbye To Retirement Traditions*, Forbes, January 26, 2013.) No one will be around long enough to receive that watch and, today, no one wears a watch so it would have to be a gold iPhone.

To share our feelings, we must have our support group in place. If you only have a partial support group (e.g. spouse), you will wear them out and they may interpret your feelings as whining. Someone in your support group should be able to hold you accountable for actions you need to take to move forward. Without this, you will be "stuck in neutral" and find it very difficult to break out. Attitude will determine how you move on. A friend once told me that "desperation has an ugly smell." He was right. When we put too much pressure on ourselves to land the next job, the desperation in our voice, body language, and anxious behavior come through to the hiring manager. Having that support group in place will reduce the desperation and hold you accountable for behaviors and techniques.

Create a budget.

This is advice that you have probably heard more than once. If you are like most people, this is one of those New Year's resolutions that you might do for a couple of months and then stop (just like the gym membership you've signed up for with the intentions of getting in shape).

We tend to spend incrementally as we increase our income. Sometimes we spend up to what we bring in and other times, we spend in anticipation of what we will earn (like counting on that commission check or bonus). Your lifestyle has probably changed since you first entered the workforce, and if there weren't sweeping changes (like winning the lottery or having a windfall of cash), it's more like ooching your lifestyle. You spend more, you make more, and then spend more, and then make more. When that revenue stream goes away, the lifestyle and associated costs do not.

You will probably hold onto the lifestyle for longer than you should, expecting that your next job will be at or above your last income. The more time that passes, the less likely this becomes and then panic sets in. Here's where the budgeting comes in.

Creating a budget will give you information on what you REALLY need to earn to support yourself and your family versus what you think you NEED. Take all of your expenses and identify them. There are some easy budget sheets you can download for free and some even have comparisons of budget to actual. Fill in the actual amounts you spend and be honest. You'll be surprised at where your money is going. You can also get support here through Dave Ramsey's Financial Peace University. Dave's program directs how to manage money which most people have to learn on their own.

Once you have a view of where you're spending your money, identify what items are "must-haves" and which are "nice-to-haves." Some items like your mortgage, food, insurance, and utilities are "must-haves." Items like entertainment, recreation, vacation, and dining out are "nice to haves." If you stripped out the "nice-to-haves," what does your spending look like? If you take the amount you need to cover your "must-haves" and divide it by the tax rate you pay, you'll get approximately what you need to make in salary. This gives you a comfort factor regarding where you need to be versus where you thought you needed to be. Here's an example:

Let's say your income was $100,000 and you were at a 28% deduction rate (this includes the deductions for taxes, Medicare, etc. Your take-home was $72,000 or $6,000 a month. Let's also assume that your "must-haves" are about $4,500 per month and the other $1,500 was disposable income for "nice-to-haves." Taking the $4,500 and multiplying by 12 is $54,000 (without deductions). Dividing the $54,000 by .72 you get $75,000. That's what you really need to cover your expenses.

If that is still too high and you want to see where else you could save, start to question the "must-haves." Can you reduce your mortgage payment to conserve cash? If you have a 15-year mortgage and you moved it to 30-year, how would that reduce your monthly expense (don't immediately do this now because you are trying to get a handle on where you NEED to be regarding income.) Can you eliminate your cable TV or go with a less expensive Internet provider? What about eliminating cable boxes that don't get used?

Question everything to see where you could get to if absolutely necessary. Bring one of your support group into this discussion, they may have practical advice on where to save especially if they have been through this exercise for themselves. You don't want to do this in a vacuum, so do your homework and have this discussion. Once you complete this exercise, your stress will go down. This exercise will provide you with a real-life view of what you need, not where the past got you.

This process of taking a step back and reviewing all of your spending may be enlightening to some people. Your outlook on borrowing and spending may change so that you keep your spending in check immediately and after you start the next chapter of your career. You may have purchased new cars in the past and now look at cars as a depreciating asset and decide to only buy used cars and those that you can purchase for cash. You may have used a credit card for purchases and switch to debit to control spending. This could be a new positive step that provides a new appreciation for "must-have" versus "nice-to-have."

Know what you really want and be patient to find it.

That might sound easy but when there is no cash coming into the household, or it's at a significantly reduced rate, or the transition is taking way too long, that desperation creeps in and you just want to go back to work and feel like you're worth something. You already are worth something, but most often we don't have the clarity of thought to really understand what we are learning at that specific moment. We probably don't understand how we can use this process to create a better version of ourselves. We get stuck thinking we want to replicate the "good old days" and just go back to how we were.

That isn't going to happen. We have to move on and that may mean reinventing yourself. To do this may require some time to consider carefully what we are good at; where we can use our talents and gifts; and who we should be talking to that could benefit from this. Naturally, we are going to think of ALL the things we can do and not "deselect" ourselves from any opportunity. If you want to go on interviews for which you know you are over-qualified, are under-qualified, have no interest in the industry, have no interest in the company, go ahead. But, if you do that, go in with the attitude that you are there to learn something, meet new people, understand more about the people, the process, the industry, anything. Just don't go in with the attitude that you HAVE to get an offer. There is a sales method that actually stresses "going for the 'no'." Now, that sounds counterintuitive but if that is your attitude, then the expectation is that

"I'm not desperate for this job." This same sales process uses an example of putting yourself in the position of having won the lottery yesterday. Do you really need this job? You're probably financial independent so what does this job really mean to you? You don't want to dismiss the opportunity and be flippant about it but don't beat yourself up either.

This process entails being honest with yourself. Your support group can be valuable here, asking you the hard questions about whether this opportunity is a good fit. Your attitude needs to reflect the belief that there is a good-fit position for you and your job is to find it. It's not the hammer and nail where, if you only have one tool and it is a hammer, everything looks like a nail.

Find where your real passion lies. Not just COULD you do the job you are pursuing but do you WANT to do the job. You may have experience in Operations, Sales, and Senior Management. Where do YOU want to be? We can sometimes fool ourselves into thinking we would really be good at a particular job just because there is an opening for this talent. It will be short-lived. You have to have some passion for what you do, or you will be wasting the talents that God has given you. Make no mistake, the talents you have were not acquired by you; they were given to you as a gift to be shared with others. Don't be like the servant that buried his talent and waited for his master's return only to return the talent without increasing the value.

Matthew 25: 14-30 The Parable of the Talents

"For it is like a man setting out on a long journey, who called his servants and delivered to them his goods.

And to one he gave five talents, and to another two, yet to another he gave one, to each according to his own ability. And promptly, he set out.

The he who had received five talents went out, and made use of these, and he gained another five.

And similarly, he who had received two gained another two.

But he who had received one, going out, dug into the earth, and he hid the money of his lord.

Yet truly, after a long time, the lord of those servants returned and he settled accounts with them.

And when he who had received five talents approached, he brought another five talents, saying 'Lord, you delivered five talents to me. Behold, I have increased it by another five.'

His lord said to him: 'Well done, good and faithful servant. Since you have been faithful over a few things, I will appoint you over many things. Enter into the gladness of your lord.'

Then he who had received two talents also approached, and he said: "Lord, you delivered two talents to me. Behold, I have gained another two.'

His lord said to him: 'Well done good and faithful servant. Since you have been faithful over a few things, I will appoint you over many things. Enter into the gladness of your lord.'

Then he who had received one talent, approaching, said: 'Lord, I know that you are a hard man. You reap where you have not sown, and gather where you have not scattered. And so, being afraid, I went out and hid your talent in the earth. Behold, you have what is yours.'

But his lord said to him in response: 'You evil and lazy servant! You knew that I reap where I have not sown, and gather where I have not scattered. Therefore, you should have deposited my money with the bankers, and then, at my arrival, at least I would have received what is mine with interest. And so, take the talent away from him and give it to the one who has ten talents. For to everyone who has, more shall be given, and he shall have in abundance. But from him who has not, even what he seems to have shall be taken away.

God will provide IF you let Him.

Too often, we ignore the messages that God sends to us (like the story *I Sent You a Rowboat*). We either believe that we are totally in control and dismiss God's plan (like the Frank Sinatra song, "My Way") or we have the attitude that there is nothing we can do, and we just accept whatever happens. The truth is somewhere in the middle. God WILL provide for us, but we have to ask (pray), have faith, recognize God speaking to us, and accept His will. We still have to practice the behaviors and techniques that will get us the next opportunity, but we aren't in control of the overall process. If you don't fight God's plan in favor of your own, be honest (the current verbiage is transparency) and try not to be something you are not, God will open the next chapter of your life for you.

Coincidences don't happen. We rationalize that something is a coincidence so we can discount the real presence of God in our life. Do you really think that everything occurs by happenstance? The odds against some of these "coincidences" would approach the odds of winning the Powerball lottery back-to-back. If you are not a religious person, God is still working in your life, and you *think* it is coincidence or luck or fate, whatever. Be open to when opportunities present themselves; be aware of the times when you choose to ignore them.

What you hear as fact is not always true.

Everyone thinks they know what is necessary to be successful. "Experts" will tell you that you won't find a job on a job board. They will tell you that those postings are already filled. Wrong. People do get hired off of job boards and you shouldn't ignore them. You can also see companies that are posting many jobs on these sites and decide if they are in a growth mode or is it a revolving door at this company?

If you do see a posting at a company that might be a fit for you, research the company to see if you have contacts who work there or have a connection to someone else there. Utilizing connections to accelerate the meeting process does not mean you are desperate for the job; it only means you're acting wisely to determine if you are a good fit for the job.

If you are a "seasoned" employee, more "mature," you probably won't have to worry about working with recruiters UNLESS you have a real specialty in a niche industry. Some recruiters work on a specific job placement and are retained by the company. They want to put qualified candidate in front of hiring managers so they can collect their fee. Other recruiters like to have repeat placements where they place someone and then place them again sometime in the future to collect another fee. Be wary of recruiters. Just like anything else, some are very good and others, not so much. Ask a lot of questions from a recruiter:

• How many candidates are you working with for this specific position? (They may be presenting multiple candidates.)

- Why do you think I would be a good fit for this opportunity? (See if they have done their homework on the position expectations, what's worked in the past, what hasn't worked, all the things you would ask in an interview.)
- Do you have an exclusive relationship with the company or are they working with multiple recruiters?
- When does your fee get paid? 30 days, 60 days, 90 days after hire?
- Is the company doing their own search as well?
- What does the hiring process look like? (Assessment testing, interviews, group hiring decision.)
- Ask the same Pain, Decision, and Budget questions you would ask in an interview. See how thorough the recruiter has been in this opportunity.

Your friends and acquaintances will all have opinions on job searching. What is really interesting is that the people who offer advice on what to do or not do probably haven't been in the job market for some time. They want to be helpful, but it's probably "head trash" and it's anecdotal. Don't dismiss the information they provide, but don't take it as fact either. Don't assume, validate.

Have another source of income beyond your spouse's income.

When you have worked anywhere for a period of time, you may get complacent. You may overvalue your worth to the company and cannot envision how they would survive without you. They can. It happens every day. An old myth held that salespeople, productive salespeople, were always the last to be let go. Not true anymore. Some companies will view salespeople like interchangeable parts, believing they can hire two brand new, young, inexperienced salespeople and let the veteran go and still be ahead. Sometimes new management could be threatened by a senior salesperson who has deep relationships with clients and needs to blow everything up, starting over fresh (especially if the current clients are all under long-term contracts that aren't up for renewal). If you became comfortable, thinking you were untouchable, you may have found yourself "in transition," looking for a new opportunity before you wanted.

Having another income source is a hedge against going through the financial crisis associated with a job loss.

It doesn't matter if you have your real estate license, flip houses, sell for a Direct Selling company (e.g. Amway, Reliv, etc.), or clean houses, whatever. The work should be able to provide a sustainable income for some period of time.

Dave Ramsey, in his 7 *Baby Steps*, describes Baby Step Number 3 as three to six months of expenses in savings. This is building a full emergency fund, and if you have this PLUS another source of income, your mental health will be much better than the desperation you may feel when looking for a job. Dave formed Ramsey Solutions in 1992 to counsel people who were hurting from the results of financial stress. He did this after he personally lost everything and went on a quest to find out how money works.

Find something that generates an alternative source of income so the reliance on your current job is decreased. The ideal income generator is one where you can "make money while you sleep." If you have to put in hours to get paid, you can only devote so many hours of your free time and the second business may not generate enough income to be worth it. We call those hobbies. Hobbies can be fun and may even generate some additional income, but this is about REAL income. If you can take your hobby and expand it and make money while you sleep, awesome.

In a blog article from Incfile.com, they provide some startling facts:

- There are 38 million home-based businesses in the U. S. (so it's more common than you think).

- Home-based businesses generate total revenues of $427 billion per year and 20% of home-based businesses make $100K - $500K per year.

- 70% of home-based businesses are successful within 3 years of founding (compared to 30% of regular businesses).

- 44% of home-based businesses are started for less than $5,000.

Look for available resources to help you align your specific talents and interests with current businesses. These kinds of guides will help you start the process. This shouldn't be an "either/or" decision, deciding if you continue to search for a job in the private sector or start a home-based business. Approaching this as an "and" will provide better decision making – looking at a home-based business as additive, not as a replacement.

Your resume is not as important as your assessment test scores.

In the not-so-distance past, your resume was your credentialing document that would separate you from the rest of the applicants. Someone would screen the resume and pass on qualified candidates to the hiring manager. From there, an interview (probably several) would take place and an offer would be made to a candidate. Not anymore. Today, your resume may not even be reviewed until a face-to-face interview and maybe not even then. The old process was to screen the resume for keywords sometimes using optical scanners to cull through the resumes. The process has changed.

Today, potential candidates are provided with a link to an assessment test to initially screen applicants. Based on those scores, a review of your LinkedIn profile and Facebook page are reviewed. The next step is a telephone interview to further screen and validate information provided, followed by more assessment testing. Narrowing down the candidates allows the interviewer to be more efficient and only sit with the most qualified candidates. Most companies are looking for a "fit." The most qualified person is not the one that is always selected. The interview process typically involves multiple interviews before meeting with the hiring manager. At that point, your resume is validated and rather than make an offer, there is a consensus and possibly another assessment that either supports or denies the subjectivity of the interviews. The process may not be this elaborate based on the level of the position and the size of the company, but even small businesses are adding the technology of assessment testing to take out the subjectivity and increase objectivity.

Prepare like you are interviewing the company because you are looking for that fit.

If you go into an interview and you are prepared to answer all of their questions, you may not find the right fit. There are all sorts of resources available online with interview questions and techniques on how to interview. You can follow these guidelines or take a very different approach. What if you took control of the interview? Not that you want to run it but at least control it. This is a different strategy, and it starts with the first introduction.

Thank the person for inviting you in – this implies you are a guest and the interviewer will take on that role. They may ask you if you would like something to drink or ask if you want to remove a jacket. They are in a host role.

Confirm the meeting – "Is an hour still good for us? Do you have a hard stop?" are ways to confirm this and not assume it's still an hour. "I'm sure you have questions for me, and I hope it's okay if I ask some questions as well." This helps set an agenda and control what is going to happen. "At the end of this interview, I assume there are two potential outcomes, one could be that we both think this is a good fit and we continue on to the next step, or we might decide that this is not a good fit and there isn't a next step." This sets up the potential outcomes rather than hoping or assuming what's next. "If I am not a good fit, I hope you'll be transparent with me and let me know that we will not move on to the next step." This gives them permission to say no and not fumble around telling you they will get back to you.

When it's your turn for questions, you want the answers to three major questions: how is the decision made; what issue does this role solve; what kind of budget are they working from. Let's take the first question on the decision process – if the person you are talking to is the decision maker, great. Most of the time, they are a screener, gatekeeper, or influencer. So how do you find out what the hiring process looks like? Ask some probing questions:

"Can you share with me what the decision process looks like? Are there multiple interviews, will this be a consensus decision or are you making the decision yourself?" This will help to understand who's involved and who's making the decision.

"Can you walk me through how this position or a similar position was filled in the past?" This will identify who was involved and who made the decision.

The second major question is regarding the position itself. Companies don't fill positions to maintain the status quo. Hiring managers are challenged to find the right person for the position. So how do you know if you are the right person? Find out what the expectation is for the position. Why is the position open? What worked well with the previous person in this position? What could have gone better? What are the biggest challenges? What are the expectations for this position? How does this position fit with the overall company goals?

There are numerous questions that could be asked based on the situation. If you have done your research on the company, you can anticipate how this position fits and what the expectations might be but don't assume. This is your opportunity to clarify and validate your assumptions. Hiring managers don't want to make bad decisions so help them to make the right one. If you can dig in on what they are really looking for and help them identify the right candidate, everybody wins. You may not be the right fit, but you won't find yourself chasing them around for a decision and having them avoid you because they don't want to tell you that they want to hire someone else.

The last series of questions is about their budget. At this point, it's not a discussion on compensation, it's more about their expectations. Are they looking to hire a top gun and were burned by hiring someone in the past with no experience? Are they looking to hire someone that they can mold into their corporate culture and, therefore, they are looking for someone with less experience? Are they looking for someone who has years of experience and can replicate what they have done in the past?

Knowing what they are looking for will help dictate the budget they have. If they want someone with experience, it's usually more expensive. Less experience may not cost as much. Are they more cost-conscience or results-conscience?

You're at the end of the interview and it's time to recap. Are you a good fit? Do you think the company is a good fit for you? You want to give the interviewer permission to be open and honest with you, and you are looking for feedback. They may try to stall you and say they will get back to you but realistically, they know now whether they would recommend moving you forward or not. This is their job, so they know. Ask. Don't be afraid of the answer. Trust in the decision and it will work out.

If you think they would be a good fit for you, tell them so and why. If you think they would be better served by someone younger, with less experience, say so. This process cuts through all of the gamesmanship and creates an honest dialogue that will benefit you in the future.

A recent whitepaper from Resourceful Manager provided *Ten Interview Questions To Weed Out The Bad Fits.*

1. How long did it take you to get here for the interview? How long would it take at rush hour? (Few people can tolerate a commute of more than an hour. They may take the job now out of desperation, but they are poor prospects long-term; and lengthy commutes are among the major reasons for turnover.)
2. What do you do for fun? (It's a good question to help you discover if they can get really passionate about something.)

3. What do you already know about our company (you may assume everyone has Googled your company's name – if they haven't, you probably don't want them) and what else would you like to know? Is there anything you really like or anything that gives you pause?

4. Where do you see yourself two years from now? Five years from now? (You'll get an idea of how ambitious they are/or how realistic they are.)

5. Tell me about a recent time when you had a substantial disagreement with your direct supervisor. How was it resolved? Now that you have the benefit of hindsight, in retrospect, who was right?

6. Tell me about a business success you're really proud of. What do you think were some of the components that led to the success? Was it a team effort? Could you have done it alone?

7. Tell me about the last time you made a significant mistake. What did you learn from the experience? (Everyone has made mistakes. If the job applicant says he hasn't, then think twice before hiring.)

8. Why do you want to work here? (Hint: if the candidate answers "to earn the good salary that you posted," you probably don't want him or her.)

9. If we talked to your last supervisor, what do you think they would say? What would they say about your outstanding qualities? What shortcomings would they probably point out?

10. You've been in the job market for a while now – where else have you applied and where else did you get past the front door?

How do we compare? Where does this opportunity rank in your mind? Where are we on a scale of one to ten? What would it take for us to be a ten?

Knowing that the interviewer has a process is important and you can set expectations for the interview when the meeting first starts but be prepared for these questions. Use examples in your response to the questions. Third-party stories are important examples of performance. Preparation in this area is referred to as: preparing "talk tracks." Talk tracks ensure you are prepared when a conversation takes a turn and you can make the transition seamlessly. One big caution is to **not** answer a question that has not been asked.

Too often we think "we're on a roll" and we have great answers to the questions being posed. Then we get carried away and start sharing information in anticipation of questions and things go south. Stick with the interviewer's process; then, ask your questions to get a feel for fit. If you have been in sales, you may have witnessed a salesperson who "oversold" the opportunity. It was right there, within their grasp, and they could not shut up. They felt compelled to say one more thing and that one more thing sent the sale sideways and ultimately out the door.

When the interviewer asks a question that you are NOT prepared for, reverse the question to gain clarity. A reversal method is to use: "That's a great question. This is obviously important for you. Can you share why this is important?" Their response will help you frame up your response without making the interview sound like a cross-examination. Some interviewers are very good at what they do and will keep control of the situation to a point where it may feel like it's less of an interview and more of an inquisition. Sometimes these are positioned to validate an assessment test score and see how you respond. Do you get defensive? Angry? Do you get quiet and unresponsive? The best advice is to be yourself and retain as much control of the interview as you can.

Everyone is looking for a fit

There's been a lot of talk about "fit." The reality is that everyone, the hiring company and the interviewees, are looking for a fit. Unfortunately, everyone struggles with what that means. You hear about "getting the right people on the bus," or "getting the right people in the right seats on the bus." The struggle is between our "feelings" (that gut feeling that tells you something is right, or it isn't) and our rational mind. We try to use psychological testing to assist us in what really is a biological issue. Our limbic brain is where our motivation lives (and the motivation of the company). Our neocortex is where our rational mind and speech reside, and the two sections of our brains don't interact that well. It's why we struggle with articulating our feelings. We try to use metaphors to illustrate our feelings but most of the time, they fall short.

Simon Sinek has studied this and has given a Ted Talk on the subject to help understand the dilemma. He has also authored two books on the subject of finding your WHY, where WHY is your motivation, why you get out of bed every morning. It's why some people can't wait to get to their job in the morning and others can't wait to leave.

Companies have a WHY, too. When your WHY and the company's WHY align, voila, FIT!

First, you should know your WHY. If you understand your own motivation and what makes you feel a part of the team, you'll be able to determine if the company is going to be a good fit for you. It's not all about ability and experience.

Here's an example: your job is eliminated, and you know people in the industry – may know them really well. You've worked with them, socialized with them and sat with them at conferences. You run in the same circles and know many of the same people. One of these people hears that you are *available*. They reach out to you and ask, "What's it going to take to bring you on board?" You are thrilled. You accept and make the assumption that this will be a good fit without doing any due diligence. Two weeks into the new job, you realize that you are not a good fit. While you have the skills and ability, the fit feels wrong. The company is a good company, but you are the round peg trying to fit in the square hole. Now, what do you do? You have to face up to your friend and tell them you're not the right person but they don't understand. They think it will work out because they know your track record. You know it's not going to work out and rather than wait six months and then make the decision, you decide to move on now before you're too far in. No one took the time to understand the WHY and if you and the new company will mesh. Now before you think this is a made-up story – this really happened.

Check out Simon Sinek on his TED Talks and his book: *Start With Why* and *Find Your Why.*

What to do when you get an offer.

Getting an offer sounds really good if you say it real fast. Before you jump in and accept, you should at least go through a process to ensure as best you can that the offer is a good decision on your part. Chip and Dan Heath in their book *Decisive*, identify four villains to making a good decision:

Widen Your Options – too often we are faced with a yes/no or this versus that decision. This is referred to as narrow framing and it leads to poor decisions. Obviously more offers are better than one, but if you only have one offer, you can still widen your options by speaking with someone who works there or someone who used to work there.

Reality-Test Your Assumptions – if you accept this offer, what's it look like? Would you be happy doing this job? Are you a good fit? What if you didn't accept? What's next? This is not a bad time to also consider how you measure performance in this position. How would you know if you are being successful? If this is a sales position, it's easier because you track closed business but what else? Part of this step-on testing is a process called "ooching" or easing into the decision. Employment decisions are typically not possible to ooch unless you are working part-time to test it or as an internship. Probably not a solution for most offers.

Attain Distance Before Deciding – this step asks you to take the emotion out of the decision and be honest. Honor your core priorities and don't compromise just to get the job. You want to remove as much "head trash" or baggage as you can so you make a rational decision.

Prepare to Be Wrong – what if you accept the offer and find out you were wrong? What's the next step? Conducting a "pre-mortem" on the job will help you determine what you would do if it doesn't work out. Would you be in a better position than you are now?

Taking some time to review the offer for more than just financial concerns and benefits will help you make better decisions.

myths

When a job elimination occurs, some of the first thoughts tend to focus on financial responsibilities. You fear you won't be able to meet your obligations and your possessions will be taken away. Only in rare cases does this really happen.

Myth #1: I will lose everything I've worked for.

Nope. Doesn't happen. Your mortgage company doesn't get notified that your job has been eliminated. Neither does the bank that has the lien on your car. The school that your kids attend don't get notified (they may find out from friends or family but unless they are concerned about tuition or re-enrollment, it probably doesn't affect them.) The utility companies don't know, the cable company, no one. If you approach this as a time to get control of your expenses, you can sit down and create a budget and really ask yourself, "What are necessities and what are luxuries?" There are apps available today to track expenses and determine where every dollar goes so you can make informed decisions to reduce debt, conserve cash or create that emergency fund.

You may not be able to refinance your house because they typically will verify employment, but you could sell off some assets that might be a burden. When you do go back to work, it's a good time to revisit your budget and set aside that emergency fund that you thought was a good idea – you just didn't have one. And, don't get into the same predicament of living above your means. Live with the budget you created. Save for specific luxuries like vacations and anticipate unexpected expenses like car repairs. The better you plan and stick to the plan, the less you will stress out if something doesn't go according to your plan.

For most people, it is easier to accept the worse than to keep a positive attitude when a job elimination first happens. Don't panic. Over the successive few weeks, when you are still able to maintain your financial commitments, your positive attitude will start to return. If you have always been in control, take this opportunity to regain control and manage your expenses. Sometimes you will want to cut back on some expenses that may not make a big impact overall but just the act of cutting back helps you feel like you are taking control. Do it. Get rid of the cable TV, eliminate entertainment like movies, dining out, whatever. Make sure you are having this discussion with your spouse/significant other. They need to understand that cutting these things out helps you feel like you are doing your part to conserve until the next opportunity comes along.

Myth #2: Your friends and family will think you are a failure.

Your spouse and your kids will NOT think this. Unless this has been the way your career has always been, they will empathize with you.

The New Normal

In a recently released study on ageism (see ProPublica, www.propublica.org/article/older-workers-united-states-pushed-out-of-work-forced-retirement), the results on job elimination are staggering. 52% of people over 50 years old will experience a job elimination. Think about that for a minute. More than one-half of all people over 50 years old will experience this. Oh and another big number from the research, 23% of this same age group will experience a job elimination more than once before the end of their work career. This isn't an anomaly, it's the new normal.

Your friends may be another story. Sometimes, your friends will not have any experience with job elimination. They won't understand how this happens. They may think that if you are skilled and experienced, why would a company let you go? Why wouldn't they look for something to keep you? Why wouldn't they negotiate a lower salary to keep your experience? These friends may see you in a different light and you'll feel it. Some may experience it themselves or they know someone close to them that it happened to and then they realize it wasn't you, it's the way companies operate in today's world.

Sometimes, the people that you thought were your friends turn out to be an acquaintance. It's okay because there will be other people in your circle that you felt were not close friends that will reach out and seriously try to help and be supportive. You will learn more about your network when a job elimination occurs.

Do not cocoon yourself and stop talking to your family. Reluctance to share what's going on with you inadvertently keeps people out. Those who are closest to you need to know. They are not your caregivers, but they are part of you, and they want to be included. The group most often overlooked is your kids. If you are in your 50's and have kids in high school, college, or maybe even married and on their own, share with them. In one example, the oldest son (in his 20's) called his dad every day at the end of the workday to check in on him. This did two things. First, it held the dad accountable to make some progress each day because he knew his son would call; and it told the dad that his son cared enough about him to be concerned, which provided an opportunity to talk one-on-one. Only a fool would attempt to do everything on their own and not share their feelings and thought process. Sharing may uncover a new idea that wouldn't be developed on your own.

Myth #3: I won't find another job.

Hogwash. You will find another job. It may take some time and it may not be easy, but you WILL go back to work. It may not be at the same compensation level as your previous job but if you were honest with what your budget should be, you'll find you can live on a lot less money by making some hard choices and changing your lifestyle. First things first: you need a budget and you must stick to it (have you heard this before? It's a recurring theme.) If you change your lifestyle to live below your prior income, when you DO go back to work, resist the temptation to go back to your old lifestyle. Stick with the budget you created. You'll have much more freedom when you aren't strapped with debt, and if another job elimination occurs, you'll be more prepared financially. Not everyone will go through another job elimination, but it doesn't hurt to plan better than you might have before.

When you are prospecting for your next opportunity, you'll have a tendency to "think small." You'll want to stay in your current industry (it's where you feel safe); you'll want the same title and same level of compensation; all because it will return you to normalcy. This may not be possible, and you'll need to keep your options open. Maybe you want to stay in the local market and not relocate. Is that a deal breaker? Know what is negotiable and what isn't. If you find a position that's a good fit and you don't want to relocate, can you commute? There are many people that commute long distances every week. They essentially live out of town during the work week and return home to family and friends on the weekend. Know what options are available and don't deselect yourself from possible opportunities.

Some people give up too soon and think they will just start their own business or go into consulting. It's not a bad idea to have options and to explore, but if you have never been an entrepreneur and didn't like the risk before, this probably isn't the time. If there is something you've been considering for some time, don't think "A" or "B," think "A AND B." Could you do both? Could you find a job where you mutually fit AND start a business part-time? Limiting your options is narrow framing and you will make poor decisions using that process.

Myth #4: Your friends will connect you with hiring managers they know.

This overconfidence may work against you. You may initially think that someone in your network, maybe a close friend, will introduce you to someone in their company or with someone they know. This may **not** happen. For whatever reason, sometimes your closest friends don't want to get involved. It could be that they don't feel comfortable recommending someone to work for their company (what if it doesn't work out), or they are unsure about your work life if they've only known you socially (maybe you're not the right employee). Your friends will try to support you by sympathizing with your situation and saying, "Let me know how I can help." They probably don't know how to help. If you press them to say, "Here's how you can help," they may resist that because of the reasons above.

One thing you should do is be prepared when someone does ask how they can help. Some friends who offer will genuinely want to help but don't know how. YOU need to have some specifics of what you are trying to accomplish and ask if they might be able to help. An example would be letting them know about a company that you are prospecting, not knowing if they may know someone there. Don't assume because you didn't see a connection on LinkedIn that they are not connected. No one is connected to everyone they know, and some people just aren't as involved in social media no matter what you read. This process could also be used for a group of your contacts, taking the pressure off the one contact you reach out to. Send a group email identifying the company you are prospecting and ask your group if anyone knows someone well enough to reach out with a request for an introduction.

If they have never been through a job elimination, they may think the problem is YOU. They're not going to ask. You may share with them that the problem is the economy, the employer, or new ownership, whatever. They will listen to your explanation, but they may not buy it. Don't be discouraged and don't be angry with them. If they haven't been through this before, they can sympathize but not empathize, and there is a difference.

Depending on your relationship, rather than relying on these friends to make introductions, use them as one of the support people you need. Maybe you have a close friend that you can share how you feel, and they can be open and honest with you. Make sure you set upfront expectations with them, so they know what role you want them to take. Tell them that you don't want their recommendation or introductions, you just want them to listen and offer objective support.

Myth #5: This won't happen again.

This is not to scare you or be "doom and gloom" but it does happen. This is more of a trend than an anomaly (see the sidebar on The New Normal). As you get closer to retirement age, it could happen again, and the job search becomes more difficult. If you have been through a job elimination, you will be more aware of your surroundings and where the company is headed. You won't assume everything will be okay even if the senior management says it will. There are those events that occur when restructuring is a given. For example, a new management team takes over, there will be changes; a merger or acquisition is being discussed, changes could occur before, during or after the event. Just be prepared. If you have another source of income and you have stuck to your budget, you'll be fine. You are never too old to find a job but when you do, the company is probably looking for your expertise and a cultural fit. That expertise must be coupled with current trends and vision.

Stay up to date on your discipline and various industries that you are prospecting. Recognize that you may be stuck in the past if you are in marketing and don't have a Twitter account; haven't posted articles or video on LinkedIn or shared a viewpoint on new marketing approaches; or if you can't have a discussion on SEO. The same goes for any discipline. You must stay current if you want to be hired for your expertise and knowledge base. If you want to build your personal brand, you have to spend some time marketing yourself. You can repost articles that you find interesting, maybe challenge your way of thinking. You can also create your own articles that position you as an expert or at least a trusted advisor that knows something about the subject you are writing. Approach this like you would approach communicating any brand to someone. If you are a big fan of iPhone or Samsung, you probably tell everyone when that subject comes up, right? So position yourself with others that when a subject comes up, that you have written about or shared an article or video, you get associated with that positioning.

Myth #6: My skills are highly marketable, and I can adapt to a new industry.

This is probably not a myth if you are 35. When you get into your 50's and 60's, your marketability goes down. It's not that you aren't valuable. You are. The problem is more related to your attitude and to a hiring manager bias. Everyone becomes less adaptable the older they get. We like stability. Learning a new industry is hard. It doesn't mean it won't happen, it's just that the skill set you have must be a fit for the hiring company. They'll look for someone who can make an immediate contribution. Approach an opportunity with humility. Your experience and past success will speak volumes. Approaching an opportunity with a "been there, done that" attitude doesn't convey adaptability.

Hiring managers sometimes have a negative bias and negative bias is more powerful than positive bias. A hiring manager who believes that, to be an asset to the company you must have industry experience, will be difficult to overcome if you don't have this specific experience. If they believe that you may not have the vitality required for the position, you may not get to the next stage in the process. Know your strengths and where you can make improvements. It could be that a company is looking for someone who understands more about the process than the product. Don't sell yourself short if you don't know the product backward and forward. There tend to be a lot of SMEs (Subject Matter Experts) running around a company so they may not need one more. Maybe what they need is a fresh set of eyes that don't come with the baggage of the industry or of a competitor. Ask yourself why you would hire YOU. What is it that a company would find invaluable in you? You don't have to toot your own horn at every opportunity or share one third-party story after another, but you want to share enough that communicates you have worked through a similar process and there were some lessons learned. Confidence is different from arrogance. Arrogant people only feel smart if someone else feels stupid. Confidence gets hired. Arrogance is shown the door.

Myth #7: The jobs posted on job boards are already filled.

This is head trash. There are real jobs on job boards, but you have to vet the opportunities. If you have been in sales, this is similar to receiving a Request For Proposal (RFP) or some potential customer wants to include you in the "bid." Some of those are real opportunities; others are not. If you approach the job listings on the job boards as just a bid and you are throwing your resume at it, it's what is referred to in sales terms as a "quote and hope." You send it your resume thinking there might be a chance, but you have no faith in the process, and it would be a miracle to move forward on this opportunity.

Why not switch up the process? You know there is the potential for a position with this company and you know the position requirements based on the job description. Rather than send in your resume and hope for the best, how about working the following process:

1.   Find a lead into the company: either the hiring manager or a friend/relative that works at the company.

2.   Ask for a warm introduction from your lead. If someone can introduce you to someone who is already working there, you can find out more about the position and whether they are looking to hire someone.

3.   In the absence of a warm introduction, contact the hiring manager and request 30 minutes to find out if this is a good fit. You can help them by not having to read through one more resume and you might help them discover what they are really looking for in this position – assuming it is real.

4.   If they don't agree to the meeting, you can either still send in your resume ("So you're telling me there's a chance" – Lloyd Christmas, Dumb and Dumber), or you can move on to the next opportunity because this may not be a real opportunity.

If you see many postings from this company and they are for multiple positions and every week, something is wrong. Companies don't keep posting positions unless they have very high turnover and can't keep employees. Do some digging before getting "happy ears" and thinking this one posting is just perfect for you.

reaching out

Asking for help is difficult. We don't like to be vulnerable. We think that reaching out is a sign of weakness. Put that aside. Deep down, people want to help. Friends, relatives and new contacts who have been through an elimination are typically more apt to help when someone reaches out. When you do reach out, have a plan. What do you want them to do specifically? Do you want advice, introductions, or a confidant who is not judgmental? Reaching out without a purpose makes it more difficult for someone to assist. Most people will meet with you but make sure you set up the meeting with expectations:

- Share the purpose of the meeting
- If you are meeting for coffee, lunch or drinks, make sure they know it is on you. Don't expect to share the cost or for them to pay. If they have been where you are, they won't let you pay anyway.
- Make it convenient for the person, both the timing and the location. Don't say that some location is not convenient. Let *them* choose.
- Check back with them before the meeting to ensure it still works for them. Things change and calendars get full. The meeting is really important for you, but they may have a thousand other things going on.

When you get a meeting, be prepared:

- Arrive early. You never want them looking around for you and you are running late. Use the Lombardi time rule: if you are on time, you're 15 minutes late.
- Set the expectations:
  ○ Thank them for meeting
  ○ Ask them how long they are good to meet. Do they have to be somewhere? Do they have a hard stop?
  ○ Reconfirm the purpose. How do you want them to help?
  ○ Tell them that at the end of the meeting there might be follow-up items that you will need to do and you will let them know they have been done; there may be a follow-up meeting and you can schedule that at the end; there may be follow-up items that they commit to and ask when it would be appropriate to follow up.
- Take notes. You won't remember everything, and if you value their advice or direction, you'll write it down.
- Commit to follow up and then do it. Let them know after the meeting that you appreciated their time and stay in touch. Let them know how it's going. Ask if you can reciprocate. Can you do anything for them?
- Remember that if you reached out to someone who has a connection to someone you wanted to meet, they may be uncomfortable doing that. As an alternative, you may ask if you can reach out and use their name as a mutual friend.

Remember Myth #4 about assuming close friends or relatives will introduce you? They may not. Don't be discouraged. These friends may have been burned in the past and, no matter how good your friendship is, they may be reluctant to make that introduction. It doesn't mean they are not a friend.

If you reach out and don't get meetings with everyone, it's okay. Some people are going to be uncomfortable with a meeting. They may not have any experience with job elimination and don't know the effects. Be patient. There are people in your network who *will* help. They don't always know that you are going through an elimination. We typically don't broadcast that event.

managing with experience

There will come a time when you start the new chapter in your career. Remember the time you spent in transition. You may be in a management position and be faced with eliminating positions. You will have the benefit of knowing the process and how to help someone mitigate the transition. You'll also know that a "blindside" is not the best method for job eliminations. Blindsides may be the least painful method for the company but not for the individual. Have compassion.

When a friend, relative, colleague, or an acquaintance reaches out to you and wants to meet, do it. If they don't know the purpose of the meeting, help them through it. Remember that they may have never had to do this before and you are now an expert. Not something you wanted to do, but you do know what works and what doesn't. Share that expertise and experience. Most people want to know that they are not alone, that someone else has been through this and can come out better.

For the most part, people who go through job eliminations are happier once they open that new chapter. They are wiser, more compassionate, more understanding and may not have accepted a position just because they received an offer. They are more in touch with their skills and values. They manage their lives with a balance that may not have been there before the job elimination. That balance includes spiritual, physical, emotional and financial.

MY STORY

 *This picture was taken in when I was the Executive Vice President of Sales and Marketing for a St. Louis based company.*

I would go on to be the COO and eventually the CEO for a new division before being eliminated.

The company had grown from $30MM when I started to $175MM when I was terminated. I was loyal to a fault and didn't see the job elimination coming.

I know firsthand what it's like to find yourself suddenly out of work and I wanted to share how I got there.

childhood

I thought my childhood was pretty typical. You know how it is when you are growing up, your neighborhood friends are just like you. No one is really a lot better or substantially worse off. All of you are from the same socioeconomic background. Your houses are pretty much the same. You don't really notice too much difference. I also attended parochial school, so we wore uniforms and that made everyone look the same. You could sense that some kids came from wealthier areas but at school, you were the same. If you're going to get bullied in a parochial school, it's probably because you're the fat kid or not as athletic or maybe not the "A" student but it won't be because you're poor.

I grew up in a suburb of St. Louis and the best comparison is to Mayberry from *The Andy Griffith Show*. We had our own police and fire departments; three grade schools and one high school. Everyone knew everyone.

My parents were hard-working people who grew up during the Depression. Neither attended high school but they worked hard. My stepdad had served in WWII as a Master Sargent in the 1st Marine Division in the Pacific theater. He enlisted when he was 16 and lied about his age. He decided not to stay on to get his pension at 20 years and was honorably discharged after 17 years. I think the war and then Korea got the best of him and he couldn't take it anymore. After his discharge, he got a job driving an oil truck that serviced residential homes in New York. He married and after his first wife lost her battle with cancer, he moved to St. Louis, though I never found out why.

My mom divorced my biological father when I was only three years old, and she met my stepdad a couple of years later. By this time, my stepdad was driving a truck for the St. Louis County Highway Department and Mom worked at the County Assessor's office. The thing about these jobs was that they were more political than most and when the pendulum swung to another political party, they reshuffled the deck. Both my parents lost their jobs, and my stepdad took a job with the local school district as a custodian while my mom got a job with a local cleaner as the front desk lady. Not the most glamorous jobs, but they were paying the bills, and I think they were happy.

My mom had the opportunity to get a job with a local Kentucky Fried Chicken franchise as the "salad lady," making salads and pies for the store. She never learned how to drive, so that limited her scope of available jobs to where she could walk, or later on, where she could catch a bus.

teen years

I began working when I was 13, raking yards for a landscaper and cutting some lawns on my own in our town. I hated yardwork and still do but I did it to earn some extra cash. The next year, I got a job with a paper delivery man and I worked before school, rolling papers and then on weekends to roll papers and make deliveries to the apartment complexes that you couldn't throw. I still remember sitting on a curb on Sunday morning, August 10, 1969, waiting to be picked up by the paper van at the end of our deliveries and reading about the Sharon Tate murders the day before.

The next year I got a job with a local pharmacy to work the soda counter, stock shelves and help the pharmacists fill prescriptions. Yes, I was filling some prescriptions because they were busy, and the rest of the store was not, and I knew how to count tablets or fill capsules. There would be all kinds of trouble today if a 15-year-old was filling prescriptions. I do remember filling bottles of Paregoric to stock the shelves in the pharmacy and an inspector was in the store and asked me if I knew what it was. I said, "Yes, it's camphorated opium." I thought he was going to have a seizure. I didn't fill any more bottles of Paregoric.

At 16, I applied for a job with Ace Hardware as a lumber cutter, working after school and on weekends to stock the precut lumber bins. Not long after that, I was "promoted" to a stock boy and then onto a buyer for the electrical department. I worked there all through high school and during my senior year, was on a co-op program to only attend school half days and work half days, so I was working 40 hours at the hardware store. I also took a job with KFC to work Sundays to make extra money to pay for my car, insurance and clothes. I bought a brand new 1971 Mustang that was on the showroom floor, but I worked all the time to pay for it.

college years

I went on to college and took jobs that paid more so I would always be searching for how to make a few more dollars. I was always looking "beyond" my current job at the next one I could get. In college, I landed a job in a grocery warehouse that was a union job. I had quit college to help pay some bills at home after my stepdad had a stroke that left him unable to work. During the period of his stroke and before his disability kicked in, we had little income in the family, so I moved home and tried to help out. My mom had quit her job because my stepdad needed 24-hour care. I ended up staying at that job and got married. I was making good money and my wife had a union job at a grocery store and with no kids, we were doing okay. It finally hit me one night when a co-worker said he couldn't wait until we were A Class (a union classification on seniority) on days. That's when I realized I could see the end of my career.

starting a family

I returned to school and became more focused. I actually landed a full-time job as an accountant without my degree and I started to go to night school. After having a job in accounting, I realized I really wasn't cut out for accounting. I had declared it as a major because most of my friends were also in accounting and I understood the numbers. I changed majors and jobs to get something in sales or marketing. I did a short stint as a manufacturer's rep, earning a small salary that would dry up pretty quickly because I was supposed to be commission-only. After six months, I was done. I had been looking for another job and landed a position with The Seven-Up Company. I started in their accounting group but after six months, managed to get into sales administration and then a field sales assignment in Louisville, KY. My wife wasn't happy about it because we had two small children and another on the way and none of our family lived out of town. We were only four hours away but that didn't matter. It turned out well for us and in 18 months, I was promoted to a larger market, Kansas City. The company was going through several changes in ownership and a friend I had worked with joined a company in Omaha selling telemarketing. She coaxed me into interviewing and so I did. I landed the job and this one was mostly commission-based so I was a little nervous, but I wasn't going to let on that I was worried. We put our house on the market, our furniture in storage and moved to Omaha, into a three-bedroom apartment with four kids. In a year, I was making more money than I had ever dreamed of. I paid off debt, bought a couple of new cars, sent the kids to private schools. The works.

I thought we were pretty happy, or at least I was. I was traveling every week and bringing home big commission checks. After a couple of years, I was more of an absentee parent. My wife wanted me to travel less and be home more to be a part of the family. I got the opportunity when the company offered me a position to run the largest division for them. So, here I was, 37 years old and running a $50 million division with all sales and operations responsibility. I thought I was kind of a big deal. I was part of the senior management team, made some changes to increase our profitability, still making good money.

A year later, we were acquired, and I took over as Vice President of Sales for the combined group. My team was doing $80 million in sales, and I was traveling to Cincinnati four times a year to review our sales strategy and execution to the Board at Cincinnati Bell. A year after that, I was given an ultimatum to move to Cincinnati or look for another job. I had already been interviewing in St. Louis and accepted a position with a local St. Louis company in the incentive business.

My career had taken a step backward, but I was living back in St. Louis and not traveling as much as I had before. We had lived in St. Louis for a couple of years when I received an offer from a smaller company ($30 million) in the same industry which I accepted.

tuition and braces

I started with the company to head up their teleservices group, but after six months, I was working for the owner and took over sales and marketing. I was back to the Executive Team and managing salespeople. We grew the company in several vertical markets and when our CFO became President, I began reporting to him—a great person with an almost impossible task of finding cost-cutting opportunities to increase our profitability. We were building a new IT platform and it wasn't cheap. He spent many late nights and weekends going through a process to find savings. In the end, he was one of the cuts that took place. He told me that it was his decision, but I wasn't sure about that. He left and the CFO that had been hired took over as COO and the owner stepped back in as President.

Over the next few years, we grew the company significantly and then in 2005, the CFO/COO was let go. I heard it was a restructuring. He was let go on a Friday night and on Saturday, I received a call to tell me that I would be the new COO beginning Monday. I retained my job running sales and marketing, but now I had all operations as well. I continued to do both jobs for eight months and then during an Executive Team meeting, the discussion turned toward what else could we do to leverage our assets and create new revenue streams. One of the ideas was to create a "wholesale" platform to enable smaller companies in our industry to utilize our platform without having to build their own platform. We would white-label the platform and they could sell it as theirs. It was decided that I would take this idea and vet the opportunity. We launched the new company and I transitioned the sales responsibilities to one of the salespeople that I had hired. I retained the COO role for the first year. We had some success with the new venture and the owner of the company asked me to focus on it full-time. I transitioned my COO responsibilities, hired a VP of Sales for the new company, and hired an Account Manager to handle our recent sales. We moved into office space away from the company headquarters to make it easier for clients to work with us and not one of their competitors.

eliminated squared

When the recession hit, we hadn't turned the corner yet on profitability and companies were not buying new incentive programs.

Also, one of our largest clients was acquired and that put a hold on using an outside resource like us. The parent company was having its own challenges. I had gone to the owner in December and told him I was thinking of buying a lake house because of the current market and interest rates. He thought it was a great idea so I really had no indication that anything would change. I received my ten-year award that January at our holiday party and the owner had great things to say about my contributions over the past ten years. Two weeks later, I closed on that lake house. We were feeling pretty good. I thought my job was solid. I had been a loyal employee who had performed well. I had stepped into roles that I had been asked to and had increased our revenues and EBITDA (Earnings Before Interest, Tax, Depreciation and Amortization.) Two weeks after I closed on the lake house, the owner called me in on a Friday afternoon and had a hired consultant tell me that my salary was going to be cut by 30%. I was blindsided. If I had known this just two weeks prior, I could have avoided buying the second home.

The following month, 25% of the workforce was let go. The 401(k) contributions were suspended, and the consultant was brought on full-time as the new CFO. A few months later, after a financial review of the new venture, the owner told me that my position was eliminated, effective immediately. No alternatives, no reductions in salary, just eliminated. I was to receive a severance package that worked out to one week for each year with the company. I was also told that the shares of the company that I had accumulated over the past eight years were also gone (there was a clause that said if you were terminated either voluntarily or involuntarily, you immediately forfeited your shares).

I was out of work, but I thought I would have a job right away. I didn't. No one was hiring, especially at my level, and companies wouldn't hire me at a lower position because they thought I would continue to look for a better job. It took me 11 months to find another job. I did some consulting during that time, but it was sporadic. We tried to sell our lake house but that didn't work so we sold our home in St. Louis and moved in with my brother-in-law, living in his basement.

I stayed with the new company for 12 months and was recruited to take over as VP Sales & Marketing for a company in Kansas City, 3.5 hours from my house. I began commuting to Kansas City every week, leaving on Sunday night or very early on Monday morning and coming back on Friday night. I commuted every week unless I was flying to a client location. I had been hired by the CEO and the Board of Managers to focus on accelerating the sales process to increase the valuation. In three years, we had increased the valuation by 60% and a new set of investors came in, bringing with them a new CEO and a new President. The former CEO became the Chairman of the Board, and I began reporting to the new President.

The President wanted me to let all of the salespeople go, eliminate all of their positions and start over. He was headed in a new direction and hired some new salespeople that reported directly to him. I asked what my role was going to be, and he wanted me to focus on our Top Ten accounts, so I did. I signed all of the accounts to long-term agreements or received extensions. In the case of our largest client, I avoided an RFP and resigned them to a new five-year agreement. As soon as that was complete, the President called me and said he had some bad news, I could move to Kansas City and take a 50% cut in salary or I could go find another job. I had been eliminated again.

I took the severance package and began my search. It took me 4.5 months of interviews to secure my next position, but it was a good fit with a company headquartered in St. Louis. There was still some travel but not like before. It was a privately-held company with great people.

I wanted to share my own story so you know that I have been in the position of a job elimination and like Jack, did not see it coming. God has a way of putting you in the right place at the right time. Sometimes, He has to hit you over the head to listen and I was one of those people that really needed to be hit in the head to realize what was going on. I decided after the second job elimination to write a book about the process and so began the journey.

If you or someone you know is going through a job elimination or is concerned about it, share this with them. I coach people that are in transition and can be reached at eliminatedjob@gmail.com. God will provide the next chapter if you let Him.

ACKNOWLEDGMENTS

I cannot express enough thanks to my friends and family for their continued support and encouragement. Without them and the people I have met along the way who shared their stories with me, this book would never have made it to paper.

To my daughter Nicole who read my manuscript multiple times and performed the first edit of the book. For a first-time author, I needed all the help I could get.

To Mary Ann Hutcherson, who encouraged me to apply for the Catholic Writers Guild Seal of Approval. I miss you and your matter-of-fact style of how to get things done. I wish you were still here to see the finished work.

I want to thank Deby Sansone Schlapprizzi for helping me understand the process for a first time author.

To Danielle Johnson for designing a cover because she knows that graphics is not my strong suit and she didn't hesitate when I asked for help.

To my kids: Nicole, Larry, Justin and Anna that knew about my job eliminations never focusing on themselves but only how they could support me.

Finally, to my caring, loving, and supportive wife, Debbie. Her encouragement when I went through my job eliminations and times got rough are what kept me going.

Made in the USA
Lexington, KY
16 February 2019